# Negotiating the European Union

# Negotiating in the European Union

## HOW TO MAKE THE BRUSSELS MACHINE WORK FOR YOU

## JAMES HUMPHREYS

CENTURY
BUSINESS

This edition first published in the United Kingdom by Century Ltd
Random House, 20 Vauxhall Bridge Road, London SW1V 2SA

Random House Australia (Pty) Limited
20, Alfred Street, Milsons Point,
Sydney, NSW 2061, Australia

Random House New Zealand Limited
18 Poland Road, Glenfield
Auckland 10, New Zealand

Random House South Africa (Pty) Limited
Endulini, 5a Jubilee Road, Parktown 2193, South Africa

Random House UK Limited Reg. No. 954009

Papers used by Random House UK Limited are natural, recyclable products made from wood grown in sustainable forests. The manufacturing processes conform to the environmental regulations of the country of origin.

ISBN 0 7126 7759 3

Typeset by Deltatype Ltd, Birkenhead, Merseyside
Printed and bound in Great Britain by
Mackays of Chatham plc, Chatham, Kent

Companies, institutions and other organizations wishing to make bulk purchases of any business books published by Random House should contact their local bookstore or Random House direct:
Special Sales Director
Random House, 20 Vauxhall Bridge Road, London SW1V 2SA
Tel 0171 840 8470 Fax 0171 828 6681

Cartoons by Banx
An earlier edition of this book was published in 1996 by the
Department of the Environment

# Contents

# Foreword

The European Community has been around for a long time. The United Kingdom first applied for membership when John F. Kennedy was President of the United States, and joined when Richard Nixon was about to begin his second term in office. Yet, in that time, the day-to-day workings of the Community have remained a mystery to the vast majority of people in Britain and elsewhere, while their importance continues to grow.

The 'cloud of unknowing' which hangs over Brussels does not only affect business people and the general public. Civil servants, too, need to know more if they are to be effective in making the Brussels machinery work, as far as possible, in the UK interest. This was the starting-point for an initiative in 1995 to improve the professionalism of the Department of the Environment in its dealings with the European institutions. As part of this, the Department wanted all officials to have access to an authoritative yet digestible guide to how the Community works, covering formal procedures and also the reality of negotiation, lobbying and deal-making which otherwise was only passed on by experience and word-of-mouth. As none existed, I was asked to write one.

The enthusiastic reaction of other government departments, MPs, academics and business people who came across that guide, titled *A Way Through The Woods*, led to this book. It has been fully revised and greatly expanded to include information on finance, grant regimes, briefing, handling the media, practical preparation, and more. There is still information here of direct relevance to civil servants, but knowing how Brussels and Whitehall work together is important for non-civil servants too: often, the only way to influence European business is through the administrations and governments of the Member States.

The one thing that remains unchanged is the idea that learning about Brussels need not be a dreary voyage to Purgatory. The text tries to be accurate; but is broken up by anecdotes, asides, whimsical introductions and cartoons to reinforce the points made and prevent the early onset of Euro-sclerosis.

This book is based to a great extent on the experiences of others, and I would like to thank colleagues in the Department of the Environment for their comments and contributions and in particular Peter Betts, Colin Bird and Graham Davis for reading the text in draft. I also had much valuable advice on specific subjects. David Earnshaw (of Smith-Kline Beecham) on lobbying; Roy Dickinson (of DGI) on Eastern Europe; David Bostock and David Prout (of UKRep) on briefing for Council and on the Parliament; Julian Farrell (of DTI) on the role of industry; and Alison Hook (of the Brittan Cabinet) on the Commission. All mistakes and omissions remain my own.

I also owe a real debt to colleagues in Whitehall, on the Environment Working Group of the Council, and above all at the UK Representation in Brussels for their advice and encouragement and for the example they provided of how to negotiate effectively, and to Simon Featherstone and Deborah Bronnert for introducing me to it all.

Finally, I would thank Charles Moseley, Elizabeth Hennessy of Random House and Michael Thomas of A. M. Heath for their encouragement, and the Rt Hon. John Gummer MP, who first had the idea of a departmental guide to negotiations and who kindly agreed that it should see the light of day in this way.

James Humphreys
February 1997

# Introduction

Dawn breaks over Waterloo, as in ones and twos the passengers for the first Eurostar train of the day to Brussels gather in the international terminal. A sprinkling of business people, lawyers and civil servants; various campaigners for cleaner bathing water, employment rights and the survival of the Great British Banger; a Euro MP returning from her constituency; the leader of a council delegation; three lords on a fact-finding mission; several scientists looking for research funding; some students doing much the same on a smaller budget.

What these people share is their objective: Brussels. But not just the city of Brussels, capital of Belgium, famous for chocolates, beer and urinating statues; their objective is also the strange collection of institutions, officials, politicians, meetings, lawyers and lunches which has the convenient label of 'Brussels'.

They also have their own, specific objectives: securing business; negotiating on behalf of the UK Government; lobbying for tougher standards, or less regulation, or no regulation at all; winning more funding; getting their points of view across; making contacts and picking up information; learning, perhaps even understanding. Not all will be successful, but as in most endeavours, those who have worked out what they want and have done their homework before setting off will have the best chance of success.

Which is where this book comes in. The United Kingdom may have been a Member State of the European Community for a quarter of a century, but 'Brussels' is still very much a mystery to most. Yet in this time, the impact of Community action has become more and more apparent. Common standards for products from cars to carrots; controls on emissions of pollutants to rivers, seas and the air; legislation to protect the health and safety of workers; protection too for wildlife and precious habitats. The pound and ounce replaced by the kilo; a blue flag flying over a Spanish beach to show the water is safe; roads and railways upgraded with

Community cash; Airbus winning more aircraft orders than the mighty Boeing; the 'CE' safety label on a toy bear. The lives of few Britons are unaffected by the EU; many now want to influence the day-to-day decision-making in Brussels.

As negotiating and influencing is about real people and real situations, let's choose at random four imaginary passengers on the Eurostar:

**Ron Noakes**

Ron is a civil servant who has just taken up a post at the Department of Trade and Industry leading day-to-day negotiations in the Council on a Commission proposal to introduce a European standard for tea-pots. Like many of his colleagues, he has never worked on European business before and, frankly, it's not his cup of tea.* It's all new, his French is pretty rusty, and he still can't make head or tail of the Co-operation procedure. But professionalism rules, and he's pushed aside his continental breakfast to start planning how to win some allies to his cause.

**Jane Maple MEP**

Miss Maple was elected to represent the Cotswolds in the European Parliament in a sensational 87% swing to the newly-formed Countrydwellers' Party. Each week, she commutes between Yew Tree Cottage, Church Lane, Hartley-on-Spode and her office in the futuristic Espace Leopold in Brussels to fight her constituents' causes. Now, over her knitting, she ponders on how to ensure that cream teas are exempted from a proposal for a new Directive on public health.

**Giles Weathervane**

Weathervane Associates represents several companies, including the manufacturers of 'Well Blow Me Are You Telling Me This Stuff's Jam!?' who are eager to expand into Eastern Europe. Giles, dynamic and thrusting, is throwing himself into securing assistance under the PHARE programme to help convert an ailing jam

---

* Only coffee is served in Council working group meetings.

factory outside Gdansk into a state-of-the-art facility for 'WBMAYTMTSJ!?'. Although his shirts are striped and monogrammed, Giles has principles: he believes in the company and the benefits the scheme will bring to local people, and even uses the product (though as an all-purpose cleaner, rather than on toast).

**Kate Queue**

Kate is a journalist with BBC Radio Nowhereshire, reporting on the efforts of the local council to win EU help to regenerate the run-down seaside resort of Gothstanton. At present, its tourist assets amount to a decrepit pier, some dowdy boarding-houses, a crazy-golf course and a donkey called Petal. Meanwhile, rumours abound that Commission inspectors have been spotted checking the quality of the bathing water, and Kate scents a scoop (perhaps enough to land her a job with Jingle FM).

---

Successful influencing – through either direct negotiation or indirect lobbying – depends first on **understanding** how the European Union works (even knowing what to call it). The first half of this book sets out the basics: the origins of the EU; descriptions of the institutions (the Council, the Commission, the Parliament and the European Court of Justice), and the procedures for adopting legislation; how the EU raises money and how it spends it. Those with a working knowledge of the EU can skip most of this or dip in to refresh their memory; otherwise, this is as painless a way of grasping the essentials as possible.

The rest of this guide is given over to **influencing** decision-making; practical preparation; devising your negotiating strategy: and then chapters on **negotiations** in the Council, working groups, committees and other meetings, the **preparation** of effective briefing material, and **lobbying** each of the institutions. The logistics of getting to Brussels (where to stay, eat and so on) are then explored, and to finish the lid is lifted off a real (well, almost real) meeting of ministers in Council.

Together, these show the way to build up and put

into action an effective **strategy** for making the Brussels machine work for you.

Finally, it is worth saying that this book is not meant as a textbook on the history or structure of the Union; or an exhaustive guide to sources of funding. It is certainly not a political tract either for or against the Union or the UK's membership. Saying 'We're in, and so we've got to make the best of it' might sound rather grudging, and it does ignore the underlying ideals and benefits of European co-operation, but it is nonetheless true. This book is an insider's guide on how to do just that.

# PART I
# THE STRUCTURE OF THE
# EUROPEAN UNION

IN THIS CHAPTER . . .
- THE ORIGINS OF THE EUROPEAN UNION
- THE TERMS EU, EC AND EEC EXPLAINED
- THE OBJECTIVES OF THE UNION
- THE SINGLE MARKET
- THE SINGLE CURRENCY

# Chapter 1
# The European Union:
# Where it came from,
# what it's for

*Let there be paper.*

## Introduction

At one point in the TV series *Yes Minister*, the Permanent
Secretary of the Department of Administrative Affairs, Sir
Humphrey Appleby, is asked what government is for. He
cannot answer, of course, because he cannot understand the
question. Government, UK-style, is not *for* anything: it just
*is*.

The European Union, by contrast, has a stated purpose: to
promote peace and prosperity in Europe by bringing its
constituent nations together. The Union is also comparatively new, and (being based on the traditions of many
nations) is rather alien to anyone brought up in the UK. This
is why those working within the European system, whether
they are lawyers, civil servants, business people or just

looking for a grant to restore their village pond, ought to know a little about its origins and its aims.

This chapter therefore introduces the European Union and its main policy areas: the creation of a single market, cohesion between regions and Member States, and policies on health, transport, industry, agriculture, the environment and so on. It then gives a potted history of the development of European integration from the aftermath of the Second World War to the formation of the Union, and in doing so concentrates on two of the key objectives of the Union: the Single Market, and Economic and Monetary Union.

## The European Union

For most day-to-day purposes, the essence is really quite simple. A treaty between the fifteen Member States establishes and governs the European Union and sets out its objectives and its powers. The Union has three constituent parts, of which by far the largest and most important is the European Community (the other parts cover security and foreign policy, and justice and home affairs). When people think of Brussels (be it curly cucumbers, bathing water standards or funds to redevelop rundown inner cities) they are thinking of the Community.

The European Community consists of:

- a **Commission** (to propose the legislation needed to achieve objectives and, together with the Member States' governments, to implement them)
- a **Council** (of ministers from the Member States, which adopts legislation and controls the budget)
- a **Parliament** (which contributes to legislation and budget control)
- a **Court** (to interpret the Treaty and Community legislation whenever necessary)

To these four could be added:

- the **governments of the Member States** (who implement

and enforce almost all Community legislation and administer much of its expenditure too)

The four central institutions are described in detail in the
next chapter, together with the other, less significant
Community bodies. At this stage, the main fact to keep in
mind is that these four institutions, together with the
Member State governments, are supposed to deliver the
objectives set out in the **Treaty** (which is, in effect, a written
constitution) through the Community's policies.

---

**What's in a Name?**
The Treaty of Rome established the **European Eco-
nomic Community** (or **EEC**) which, being based upon a
**common market**, was often described as such. In the
1980s, the EEC merged formally with the European
Coal and Steel Community and Euratom to form the
**European Community** (so that the EEC became the **EC**).
Finally, the Maastricht Treaty created new areas of
European co-operation in parallel with the existing
Community: together, the larger body is called the
**European Union**: the European Community continues
to exist within the **EU**.

So, to recap, the terms EEC and Common Market are
redundant, marking stages on the road to the current
EC, which is itself part of the EU. The terms Community and Union are used pretty freely in the rest of this
guide.

---

## Community Policies

The broad aims of the European Community are set out in
Article 2 of the Treaty, which states that the task of the
Community is to promote

a harmonious and balanced development of economic
activities, sustainable and non-inflationary growth
respecting the environment, a high degree of convergence of economic performance, a high level of
employment and of social protection, the raising of the

standard of living and quality of life, and economic and social cohesion and solidarity among Member States.

These aspirations are to be met by means of a single market, by Economic and Monetary Union, and by the implementation of a series of policies set out in later articles of the Treaty. This elevation of the Single Market and monetary union above all other policies is not accidental: the common market is the most vital part of the Union by some way, while EMU – if and when it happens – is likely to be just as important. These two are dealt with below in considering the origins and development of the EU.

More detailed objectives are set out in individual articles in Part Three of the Treaty, including the provisions on the Single Market and EMU discussed above. Seventeen 'titles' contain provisions on the main areas of Community activity:

| | |
|---|---|
| Title I | Free movement of goods |
| Title II | Agriculture |
| Title III | Free movement of persons, services and capital |
| Title IV | Transport |
| Title V | Common rules on competition, taxation and approximation of laws |
| Title VI | Economic and monetary policy |
| Title VII | Common commercial policy |
| Title VIII | Social policy, education, vocational training and youth |
| Title IX | Culture |
| Title X | Public health |
| Title XI | Consumer protection |
| Title XII | Trans-European Networks |
| Title XIII | Industry |
| Title XIV | Economic and social cohesion |
| Title XV | Research and technological development |
| Title XVI | Environment |
| Title XVII | Development co-operation |

This provides an impression of the scope of Community action, for the Community may not act in a policy area unless given the power to by the Treaty. It is also worth noting that not all policy areas are equal: they can be divided up according to the respective roles of the Community and the Member States.

In some areas (such as agriculture, fisheries and international trade), the Community takes the lead in policy formation, and these are described as **common policies** (hence the Common Agricultural Policy).

In other areas (social, environment, overseas development) the Community and the Member States each act, and for these areas the Community has **policies**.

Elsewhere (such as education, training, consumer protection and health), the Community only makes a **contribution** to policies which remain predominantly the responsibility of the Member States. This ties in with the concept of subsidiarity: Article 3b of the Treaty states that, in accordance with this principle, where responsibility is shared between the Community and the Member States, the Community should only act if the objectives of the proposed action cannot be achieved at the level of the Member States *and* can be better achieved at the Community level.

---

**Is It All This Dull?**
Some words of comfort to those desperate for some anecdotes about real negotiations, or bankable lobbying tips: these will follow. Spanish monkeys dance on p.73; whisky bottles are passed round by ministers on p.210, and Hell's Angels besiege the European Parliament on p.193.

---

## The Origins of the European Community

The origins of European integration can be found in the aftermath of the Second World War. The war had left Europe devastated: millions of people were refugees, threatened by starvation, while factories and infrastructure were damaged or destroyed. At the same time, most people saw the war as proving the failure of the pre-war order. Europe would have to be rebuilt: physically, socially and politically. Above all, security and so prosperity required a lasting reconciliation between Germany and France.

This gave rise to several initiatives which sought to link the political and military interests of the Western European states. Some, such as the European Defence Community, came to nothing. Others, such as NATO, remain to this day. At the same time, politicians and intellectuals saw the need to link economic interests too. They reasoned that if their economies became sufficiently interdependent, war between European states would become 'not only unthinkable but also materially impossible'.

They began with the strategic industries of coal and steel: hence the European Coal and Steel Community (ECSC), set up in 1951, which gave supra-national powers over these industries in Belgium, France, Germany, Italy, Luxembourg and the Netherlands. The same thinking lay behind the establishment in 1957 of the European Atomic Energy Community (Euratom). Both promised greater security: they also allowed the development of these industries to be planned rationally, above national competition and subsidy.

### Free Trade or Common Market?

Crudely, goods produced in one Member State of a free-trade zone are exempt from duties when imported into another, but import controls and the associated paperwork are still needed to prove the origins of the goods. Otherwise, goods could be imported into one Member State with a low import duty, then shipped into another with higher import duties, so evading the higher rate. Also, goods part-manufactured outside the zone are only entitled to a proportionate part of the exemption. Barriers and bureaucracy remain, and so, in practice, a free-trade area could never form the basis of a true single market for goods and services.

A customs union, by contrast, removes all import duties between Member States *and* has a single external rate of duties, so that goods entering all countries pay the same duty. There is no need to prove the origin of goods and so internal controls can be removed entirely.

Then, in theory, a manufacturer can compete on equal terms with competitors even if the wrong side of an internal frontier, because the frontier exists on paper only. A true single market, and the economic benefits it brings with it, then becomes possible.

The great economic prize, though, was to remove the brake on economic growth of customs duties and other controls between Member States. These duties could be eliminated by two routes: the creation of a free-trade area; or of a customs union. The difference between these two options is at once arcane (see box) but also crucial: it explains, for example, why the United Kingdom was unwilling to join the European Economic Community in 1957, but was a founder member of the European Free Trade Association in 1960. In essence, the customs union implied greater economic and political union than a free-trade area. It was precisely because of the additional political dimension that it was attractive to those in Europe pressing for greater integration.

## The Treaty of Rome

So in 1957 the six members of the ECSC formed the European Economic Community and began the process of removing internal duties and other barriers and harmonising the external tariff. Over time, the Commission of the EEC and the European Court of Justice took on the leadership of this process. At the same time, policies for agriculture, industry and limited regional development were implemented.

In terms of political integration, though, the EEC did not deliver as much as was expected by its founders: in particular, the confrontation between the EEC and France in the mid-1960s limited its supra-national character. Progress by unanimity slowed the growth of the EEC: this problem worsened after the accession of Denmark, Ireland and the UK in 1973.

The 1970s were dark, dreary years for the EEC, and the

economic slump fuelled by the oil crises of 1973 and 1979 did not help. The main policy development was a plan to move towards a single currency through the European Monetary System and the Exchange Rate Mechanism (ERM), but currency market volatility prevented the locking of exchange rates.

## The Single Market

The Treaty set up a common market for goods and services, and the original twelve-year deadline for removing internal tariffs was met comfortably, but creating a customs union was only a stage on the road to a truly unified market. Even in a common market, products cannot move freely across national borders unless other barriers have been removed too:

- Physical barriers, such as customs checks, which delay shipments
- Legal barriers, such as product requirements based on different technical standards
- National discrimination, such as state enterprises buying only home-made products

Despite the efforts of the Commission and the European Court of Justice in the 1960s and 1970s, many such barriers remained. In the 1980s, this led to the idea of a second 'big bang', whereby popular and political enthusiasm could be mobilised to sweep them away at one go: what became the '1992 Project'.

The Single Market was more ambitious than just improving the common market in manufactured and agricultural goods: it also sought to make a reality of the commitment in the Treaty to the free movement of persons, services and capital (together known as the **four freedoms**). Not only would truckloads of TVs, toasters and apples sail past disused customs posts without slackening speed on their way from one market to another, but Danish architects would be able to work in Greece, Dutch insurance companies would be able to sell life assurance in the Belgian market, and British conglomerates would be able to move funds between subsidiaries in different Member States without being subject to exchange controls.

The 1992 campaign therefore had three targets:

- Removal of customs barriers (including introducing the new procedures for Value Added Tax and intra-Community trade statistics so beloved of small business)
- Harmonisation and/or mutual recognition of product standards, professional qualifications and other business rules (including effective policing of rules against spurious national standards as hidden barriers to trade)
- Ending practices such as encouraging 'national champions', subsidising strategic industries, favouritism in awarding contracts and other overt and hidden state aids to domestic industries

Implementing the single-market project needed three hundred pieces of European legislation, and this built up pressure to streamline the decision-making process by extending the use of Qualified Majority Voting (QMV). Under this system, one Member State alone cannot block the adoption of legislation: several states need to vote against, using weighted votes (ranging from ten for the four largest states down to two for Luxembourg). This wider use of QMV – and new powers for the European Parliament – was brought into the Treaty by the Single European Act of 1985.

This reform proved effective, and all but a handful of the legislative acts were in place by 1 January 1993, but the impact of the Single Market on Europe's business community is ongoing, as companies adjust to operating across the Community and expand or rationalise, merge or set up joint ventures. As with the first moves towards a common market, its full development will take time, and many 'users' wonder if it really exists. Its champions in the UK are business groupings (such as trade associations and the Confederation of British Industry) and government (the Department of Trade and Industry has a Single Market Compliance Unit to investigate apparent breaches of its provisions): in Europe as a whole, their opposite numbers, together with the European Commission and the European Court of Justice, carry the torch.

---

**A True Single Market?**
The extent of the success of the Single Market is a matter of judgement: French ministers still seem to drive around exclusively in Citroëns, Renaults and Peugeots, yet the Great British Taxi-cab may now be sold and ply for hire on the streets of Paris.

---

## The Creation of the European Union

Even before 1992, though, pressure for further integration led to another Inter-Governmental Conference of the Member States, which culminated in the 'Treaty on European Union' signed in Maastricht in 1991. Once again, majority voting was extended and a new legislative procedure, which gave the European Parliament the right to veto some legislation, was introduced. Symbolically, the Treaty explicitly conferred joint citizenship on the people of Europe, to match their tangible rights to live and work in any Member State. Most significantly, the Treaty set out a timetable to lead towards Economic and Monetary Union in Europe.

---

**Inter-Governmental Conferences**
Since the mid-1980s, Treaty revisions have been carried out not by the Council on a proposal from the Commission, but by the Member States meeting as independent countries (hence inter-governmental conferences).

---

The Maastricht Treaty also included, for the first time, Justice and Home Affairs and a Common Foreign and Security Policy as areas of European business, within the European Union. Fortunately, at present these areas are very much the territory of experts, even within national civil services, and little more needs to be said about them. The reason for this, and the reduced role for the Community institutions, is that both areas are seen as more sensitive than the business transacted by the Community: Justice and Home Affairs includes policy on police co-operation, immigration, anti-terrorism measures and the like, while CFSP is about tanks, atom bombs and peace-keeping missions. Serious stuff.

What is less serious is the bizarre Euro-analogy (© *Foreign and Commonwealth Office 1990*) widely used to describe the Union, which is compared to a temple with three pillars. The first pillar is the Community, the second JHA, the third CFSP, and together they make up the Union. (Clearly a temple with no roof, then.) The vast bulk of EU business still takes place within the EC pillar.

## Economic and Monetary Union

The provisions for Economic and Monetary Union in the Treaty are an example of *future law*: binding, but not yet. The Treaty contains a timetable for the introduction of EMU which cannot be altered except through a revision of the Treaty. Only two Member States – Denmark and the United Kingdom – can choose whether to participate; the other Member States will, if they meet the appropriate criteria, join a single currency (to be known as the Euro) and, even more significantly, align their economic and monetary policies.

Those who support monetary union point to the advantages. The costs of converting currencies are heavy enough: they are much worse if a business has to cover possible changes in exchange rates too. A currency fluctuation of, say, 10% could easily wipe out the entire profit margin on a contract. Covering this can make a foreign company uncompetitive compared to one doing business in its own market and so insulated from currency risks. On a larger scale, one Member State of a single market could gain a competitive advantage over its neighbours and competitors by means of a devaluation of its currency. At its heart, the single currency is seen as bringing Europe closer together politically and socially.

What is not clear is whether EMU will work; and the scale of other changes which would follow if it did. As it has yet to happen, these exciting questions can be ducked. Instead, see the timetable for EMU below.

---

**Countdown to EMU**

The Maastricht Treaty on European Union set an outline timetable for Economic and Monetary Union, leaving the detail (such as the name the 'Euro') to subsequent Council acts.

All Member States which meet the convergence criteria* are committed to participating in EMU, except for Denmark and the United Kingdom who may choose not to do so.

**1 January 1994**
Member States prepare for EMU. The European Monetary Institute, based in Frankfurt, is established.
**Early 1998**
The European Council determines which Member States meet the convergence criteria and so qualify for EMU. The European Central Bank is then be established and begins work on coins, banknotes and so on.
**1 January 1999**
The Ecu (European Currency Unit) formally becomes the Euro. Exchange rates between the Euro and the participating Member States are fixed irrevocably. The European System of Central Banks, combining the European Central Bank with the central banks of the participating Member States, is then established. The

* The convergence criteria are based on the premise that a single currency can only be introduced successfully when the economies of the participants are broadly in step in terms of key indicators such as inflation and public debt. The criteria are:
– inflation within 5% of the three best Member States
– bond yields within 2% of the three best Member States
– budget deficit must not exceed 3% of Gross Domestic Product;
– gross public debt must not exceed 60% of Gross Domestic Product;
– exchange rates to be within the normal Exchange Rate Mechanism fluctuation margins for the preceeding two years.

---

Euro is used thereafter for issuing public debt; and for other transactions by companies or individuals on a voluntary basis.
**1 January 2002**
Full introduction of the Euro, including bank accounts, notes and coins, and phase-out of national currencies over six months.

## The Future

The Market/Community/Union continues to evolve: the IGC which began in 1996 is unlikely to be the last, while enlargement in all directions and particularly to the east is foreseen. As before, expansion raises questions about institutional reform; the pace of European integration (would widening through enlargement prevent the Community from deepening through greater integration?); and the need for Member States to move at the same pace (described by a series of clichés: *multi-speed Europe, fast-lane membership, concentric circles, variable geometry*). Discussing how it might develop, though, is well beyond the scope of this guide. The following chapters, however, may help you to shape it yourself.

# Chapter 2
# The Institutions of the European Union

*The guards led Bond across the vast underground cavern, past the pool full of sharks, to where a man sat at a control panel, staring at a bank of TV screens and stroking a white cat.*

*'Blofeld!'*

*'Yes, Mr Bond, we meet again. But now the advantage is mine.'*

*'But why have you brought me here?'*

*'To explain my plan for world domination, of course. You see, SPECTRE has infiltrated the Council of Ministers, has men and women placed within the Commission, has even managed to find out where the Court of Auditors is based. And now, with the world's largest computer, we have cracked the secret of the Parliament's internal procedures.'*

*'But why?'*

*'Power, Mr Bond. Together, all this gives me more power than ten thousand of your puny atom bombs. And I mean to use that power.'*

*'You're quite mad, Blofeld. You'll destroy the world!'*

*'On the contrary, Mr Bond. I shall create a new one!'*

## The Institutions

The Union consists of four main institutions: the Commission, which proposes the legislation needed to achieve the objectives set out in the Treaty and shares administration with the Member State governments; the Council, which adopts the legislation; the Parliament, which has certain powers over adoption and over the budget; and the European Court of Justice, which decides disputes between the institutions and with the Member States.

## The European Commission

The Commission is a confusing term. There are twenty Commissioners, appointed by the Member States but charged with a higher loyalty to further the goals of the Union and implement and uphold its legislation. Formally, this is 'the Commission', though it is sometimes referred to as the 'College of Commissioners' to distinguish it from the Commission Services. The Services are civil servants who carry out the instructions of the Commission and are the 'meddling Eurocrats' of legend.

The Commission's job is to initiate the actions necessary to further the objectives in the Treaty (set out in Chapter 1) and then see that they are done. To this end it has the sole right to propose legislation (known as the *right of initiation*) and also has a duty to see that Community law is enforced and to take action (known as *infraction proceedings*) against breaches by individuals, companies and even Member States (see Chapter 4). It has certain administrative and monitoring functions, such as overseeing expenditure and setting standards, but most of the actual business of implementing Community programmes and laws is carried out by the Member States' own civil services.

Each Member State appoints one Commissioner, except France, Germany, Italy, Spain and the UK, who appoint two. The Commission term is five years (the current Commission changes at the end of 1999). The Commissioners are allotted portfolios (agriculture, research, environment and so on) by the President of the Commission, who is appointed by unanimity by the Council. Decisions are usually taken by consensus: where this is not possible, only a simple majority (eleven 'votes') is necessary to make a decision. If a Commissioner cannot attend a meeting of the college, an official from his or her office (*cabinet*) may attend and speak if asked to do so, but, unlike Permanent or Deputy Ambassadors in the Council, may not vote in the Commissioner's stead.

---

### The Current European Commission

| | | |
|---|---|---|
| Jacques Santer | (Luxembourg) | President |
| Sir Leon Brittan | (UK) | Trade and Asia/US |
| Manuel Marìn | (Spain) | Mediterranean |
| Martin Bangemann | (Germany) | Industrial policy |
| Ritt Bjerregaard | (Denmark) | Environment |
| Emma Bonino | (Italy) | Consumers and fisheries |
| Hans Van den Broek | (Netherlands) | Foreign policy |
| Edith Cresson | (France) | Research and training |
| Joao de Deus Pinheiro | (Portugal) | Africa/Pacific |
| Franz Fischler | (Austria) | Agriculture |
| Pàdraig Flynn | (Ireland) | Social policy |
| Anita Gradin | (Sweden) | Immigration and fraud |
| Neil Kinnock | (UK) | Transport |
| Erkii Liikanen | (Finland) | Budget |
| Mario Monti | (Italy) | Internal market |
| Marcelino Oreja Aguirre | (Spain) | Institutional affairs |
| Christos Papoutsis | (Greece) | Energy and tourism |
| Yves-Thibault de Silguy | (France) | Economics |
| Karel van Miert | (Belgium) | Competition policy |
| Monika Wulf-Mathies | (Germany) | Regional policy and TENs |

Sir Leon Brittan and Manuel Marìn are also Vice-Presidents of the Commission.

---

The European Parliament sanctions the appointment of the Commission, holding hearings to cross-question Commissioners on their views and policies, and has the power to reject the proposed Commission as a whole, but not individual Commissioners. The EP can also subsequently dismiss the Commission, again as a whole. Neither power has yet been used, but both have been threatened.

## Cabinets
Each Commissioner is assisted by a 'cabinet': a group of usually six to eight officials who carry out the wishes, or the inferred wishes, of the Commissioner in a series of formal meetings and informal contacts with each other, the Services and other institutions. The cabinet is appointed by the Commissioner on a personal basis, though all are Commission officials. A typical cabinet is headed by the *chef de cabinet* and would contain one or two political assistants; one or two experts in the area for which the Commissioner is responsible; one or two officials who understand the Community system from the inside; one or two from the civil service of the Commissioner's Member State; and a press officer (sometimes known by the French term *porte-parole*).

Cabinets deal with the business arising from the Commissioners' portfolios and also their political business, such as correspondence and speech-writing. Each cabinet member is also responsible for a range of subjects on which other Commissioners take the lead.

Cabinets are usually named after the Commissioner, so in any Brussels restaurant you will overhear conversations beginning 'I spoke to the Kinnocks about this' or 'Can we square the Bangemanns?'

## Chefs' Meetings
When a proposal is to be put to a meeting of the Commission, the members of each cabinet who deal with the subject meet in the week before (usually Thursday or Friday) to consider the proposal, which is presented by the members of the lead cabinet with support from officials from the lead Directorate-General of the Commission Services. These are known as 'chefs' or sometimes 'special chefs' meetings, each taking the title of the subject area (hence, 'state aid chefs', 'environment chefs'). The meetings will either:

- Pass the proposal to the next level; or
- Hold it over for further consultation and/or amendment; or
- Send it back to the Commission Services for further work

The next level is the weekly meeting of 'chefs de cabinet' or 'hebdo chefs': that is, the weekly (in French, *hebdomadaire*) meeting of the heads of each cabinet held (usually on Mondays) to prepare the work of the meeting of Commissioners (usually held each Wednesday). The chef de cabinet and Commissioner meetings are similar to Coreper and Council (see below, p 31) in that only those items which could not be agreed at the lower level are discussed: all others are included on the agenda but are usually put through on the nod.

When one or more cabinets place a reserve on a proposal which cannot be resolved in bilateral contacts, the dossier would go to the weekly chefs' meeting. If it cannot be sorted out even there, then the matter would go for discussion at the weekly meeting of the Commission.

### The Written Procedure
As an alternative to the above system, a proposal can be put through by a written procedure. The same process of reserves and negotiations applies: the details of the procedure are not of particular importance (or interest).

### Commission Services
The Commission Services are divided up into Directorates-General (DG I to DG XXIV), each headed by a Director-General, with its own responsibilities and administrative structure.

| Functions of each Commission Directorate-General | |
|---|---|
| I | External relations: US and Pacific |
| IA | External relations: Central and Eastern Europe and the CSFP |
| IB | External relations: Mediterranean, Middle East and Latin America |
| II | Economic and Financial Affairs |

| III | Industry |
|-----|----------|
| IV | Competition |
| V | Employment and social affairs |
| VI | Agriculture |
| VII | Transport |
| VIII | Development |
| IX | Personnel |
| X | Information, media and culture |
| XI | Environment |
| XII | Research and development |
| XIII | Telecoms |
| XIV | Fisheries |
| XV | Internal market and financial services |
| XVI | Regional policy |
| XVII | Energy |
| XVIII | Credit and investments |
| XIX | Budget |
| XX | Financial control |
| XXI | Customs |
| XXII | Education, training and youth |
| XXIII | Tourism |
| XXIV | Consumer policy |

The Directorates and Units are headed by Directors (usually A2 grade) and Heads of Unit (usually A3 grade) respectively. Lower down the hierarchy, the main posts are Administrator (A6–7) and Assistant Administrator (A8). There are also personal appointments, such as Adviser to the Director-General.

**Commission Grades**
The Commission grade structure has four cadres or grades:

A: Administrators
B: Assistant Administrators
C: Administrative/clerical support staff
D: Cleaners, drivers and other support staff

The A and B grades contain several types of employee:

- Fonctionnaires (permanent staff employed by the Commission)
- Agents Temporaires or Temporary Agents (ATs: employed by the Commission on contracts of up to three years)
- Auxiliaires (consultants – in theory self-employed – working on specific projects, but sometimes used to avoid staffing restrictions)
- Detached National Experts (DNEs: officials from the Member States' administrations, working for the Commission on contracts of up to three years: salaries are paid by the home administration and expenses by the Commission)
- Stagiaires (employed by the Commission for five-month 'stages': nominally a form of work experience, though some stagiaires are given more valuable or responsible work)

A-grade officials are subdivided: A1 to A8. Promotion tends to be by a mixture of time served, personal performance and (at the higher levels) political influence and national quotas.

The Commission usually develops policy much as in the British civil service. Heads of Sector and Heads of Unit formulate policy: individual desk officers draft proposals; this passes up through the hierarchy for modifications. There are, however, differences and these should be kept in mind in particular when planning or seeking to influence a proposal:

- Individuals within the system have more latitude to develop policy according to their own judgement.
- The cabinets often play a role both in inspiring policy and in influencing proposals emerging from the Services.
- There is much less co-ordination of policy within DGs or with other DGs (although all significant proposals must be cleared with other interested Directorates-General through a process known as *inter-service consultation*).

**Recruitment to the European Civil Service**
Posts in the Services of all the institutions tend to be well paid by UK civil service standards (though not when compared to some other European administrations or international bodies such as the UN). The work is also often highly challenging and demanding, and for these reasons (let's not say which is more important) the number of people wanting to work in 'Brussels' far exceeds the number of posts. The recruitment procedure is therefore long and rigorous (though it tends to favour those who write good essays rather than who are good managers). The stages are:

(1) Pre-qualification: only applicants who meet certain criteria (age, qualifications, nationality) may apply.
(2) All applicants sit a written test of their general knowledge: 90% or so are then eliminated.
(3) The survivors sit a day-long series of written tests, mainly based around essays but with a language paper too. Those failing any one of these papers are eliminated.
(4) The final stage is an interview (in two languages).

For many, the prize is worth the effort. Help for UK applicants (who in the past have not done very well in these tests) is provided by the European Staffing Unit, part of the Cabinet Office. The address is in Appendix III.

*The Secretariat-General*
This is the central bureaucracy of the Commission (and not to be confused with the Council Secretariat). It carries out certain co-ordinating tasks (such as transmitting formal documents and recording the implementation of legislation by Member States), though inter-service co-ordination is mainly achieved at Director-General and cabinet levels: when heads really need to be knocked together, the cabinet of the President of the Commission would intervene.

The Secretariat-General also carries out functions which do not fit easily into a particular DG. It is, for example, the home of the Human Resources Task Force and the Europol liaison secretariat, and leads on horizontal issues such as subsidiarity and deregulation.

### The Commission Legal Service

This body of lawyers provides legal advice within the Commission and prepares formal infraction proceedings (see Chapter 4). They do not report to individual Directorate-Generals but to the Commission as a whole, and so their advice often runs counter to the wishes of parts of the Commission. This said, their advice tends to be Commission-friendly and may also influence the thinking of the Council Legal Service. The latter provides the same function for the Council (see p. 28 below) and the two bodies often discuss issues and so influence each other.

## The Council

The main roles of the Council are to agree the legislation needed to achieve the Community's objectives and to represent directly the interests of the Member States.

Go to a meeting of the Council and it seems clear that it is the second which takes precedence. Ministers sit behind the name-plates of their countries; speak in their national languages; argue the case for their Member State. Yet the Council is also an institution of the Union, and the interests of individual Member States are often placed below the interests of the Council or the Union as a whole.

This is most clearly seen in the practice of decision-making by majority voting rather than unanimity, so that no Member State has a veto as such. Also, in its dealings with the European Parliament, the Council often seeks to protect its powers by acting as a single body even if there would be a short-term advantage for individual Member States in making common cause with the EP.

The Council's work is prepared by diplomats and officials in a committee called **Coreper** and in less formal **working groups**. These bodies are part of the wider institution known as 'the Council'. As it is in this institution that legislation is negotiated line by line through to adoption, its importance cannot be overstated.

A Council meeting consists of representatives from each of the Member States: either Ministers, Permanent Representatives (Ambassadors), or their Deputies. The Commission is represented by the appropriate Commissioner, Director-General or, rarely, another Commission official. The meetings are chaired by the Presidency, which each Member State holds for six months (starting on January 1 and July 1) in turn (see box for the order of rotation).

---

**Order of Presidencies of the Council until 2004**

1997   Netherlands (1 January–30 June)
       Luxembourg (1 July–31 December)

1998   United Kingdom
       Austria

1999   Germany
       Finland

2000   Portugal
       France

2001   Sweden
       Belgium

2002   Spain
       Denmark

2003   Greece
       Italy

2004   Ireland
       Netherlands

---

The Commission and Presidency always sit at the two ends

of the table. Each delegation has three seats (for the Minister, the Ambassador or his Deputy, and the lead policy official) at the main table and another three seats behind. On these same dates, the Member States all move one place to the left and so one place nearer to taking up the Presidency seat.

## The Council Secretariat

The Council, and in particular the Presidency, is assisted by a cadre of officials known as the Council Secretariat (formally, the Secretariat-General of the Council). Secretariat officials advise the Presidency on the handling of Council business, prepare Council documents (including revisions to legislative proposals and possible compromise texts) and generally help the process along. The Secretariat is divided into Directorates which shadow one or more Councils, and its formal role is to:

- Set up and administer Council meetings
- Assist in preparing documents, including draft legislation
- Prepare minutes of Council meetings
- Translate documents and interpret in meetings
- Run the Council buildings

The Council Secretariat has just over 2,000 staff (including translators and interpreters) so does not have many officials working on the first three of these tasks. For example, there might be only three or four officials supporting the Internal Market or Social Affairs Councils. Although discreet and impartial (they do not represent specific Member States), Secretariat officials are important and influential players in negotiations. The Secretariat also includes a **Legal Service**, which provides impartial legal advice to the Council, Coreper and working groups.

## The Permanent Representations

The Council also relies on the work of the Permanent Representations to the European Union of each Member State. These are in effect embassies and provide the diplomats who attend Council and also the Council committees and working groups. The Permanent Representative (equivalent to an Ambassador) and the Deputy Permanent Representative lead Coreper, while attachés covering the work of each Council sit on the working groups. The United Kingdom Permanent Representation (known as UKRep) is described more fully in Chapter 9.

## The Workings of the Council

The Council of Ministers is, in theory, one body: the Industry Council could, for example, adopt a Directive on Migratory Birds. In practice, other Councils do this only where there is no need for discussion of the proposed measure. This gives rise to the system of 'A' and 'I' points for uncontroversial business. Otherwise, dossiers are dealt with by the relevant Councils, though the exact distribution of dossiers between Councils falls to the Presidency of the day.

---

**Earth-Moving Machinery**

The Commission's 1993 proposal to revise the Directive on Noise Emissions from Earth-Moving Machinery had to be adopted to a tight deadline. The original Directive was adopted in the Internal Market Council, but the IMC working group was fully occupied under the Belgian Presidency. So the Belgian industry attaché had a word with his environment colleague, who had a free slot that week. The proposal was negotiated in the Environment Working Group and adopted by the Environment Council. History may be full of 'what ifs?': another to add to the list is how different the Directive would have looked if agreed by Industry Ministers rather than Environment Ministers.

---

The Council is governed by rules of procedure. From time to time these affect the business in the Council significantly: for example, under Article 2.2 of the rules, a Member State can insist on a vote at Council only if it adds the item to the agenda at least sixteen days before the meeting. Miss the deadline and another Member State might insist that a decision cannot be taken.

**The Main Councils**

| | |
|---|---|
| Agriculture | Internal Market |
| Budgets | (Overseas) Development |
| Culture | Regional |
| ECOFIN (Economics and Finance) | Shipping |
| Environment | Social Affairs |
| Fisheries | Telecoms |
| General Affairs (including Foreign Affairs) | Transport |
| Health | Youth |
| Industry | |

The main Councils meet regularly (for example, the Social Affairs and Environment Councils meet four times a year): Council meetings in June and October are held in Luxembourg and meetings in other months in Brussels. The frequency and exact dates, the length of the meetings (usually one or two days) and, for practical purposes, the bulk of the agenda are set by the Presidency. The programme of Council meetings is usually roughed out two or three Presidencies ahead and the agenda for individual Councils discussed and agreed by Coreper between two and three weeks in advance.

At Council, it is usually not physically possible for all members of a delegation to sit in the Council chamber, and a separate room (the *salle d'écoute*) is available, where the proceedings are shown on TV with simultaneous translation. Coreper and working groups follow the same pattern (except that they do not have salles d'écoutes). Occasionally, when the subject is particularly sensitive, the Council may go into **restricted session** with only the Minister and one other official allowed into the Council chamber.

Council meetings are usually private, although recently there has been a little more openness: some set-piece debates have been relayed to a room open to the public. Oddly, attendance has been sparse at many of these events.

*Informal Councils*
In addition to the formal Councils, Presidencies may hold informal Councils in their own country. These usually consist of a semi-formal ministerial meeting to discuss one topic (an example is 'Tourism and the Environment' held appropriately on the sun-drenched Greek island of Santorini) and a series of social events (visits to historical monuments, receptions, sailing trips).

Informal Councils (more properly, informal meetings of Ministers of Trade or Agriculture or whatever of the Member States) cannot take any decisions or pass any legislative acts. However, the host Presidency usually produces a communiqué (known as Presidency conclusions) and may try to get Ministers to sign up to it. This can pose problems: Presidencies have been known to use the relaxed, informal atmosphere to try to approve conclusions which would commit the Council to certain actions (usually spending money on the pet projects of the Presidency).

Participation at informals is usually limited to the Minister; one or two policy officials on the theme of the informal; one or two co-ordinators; the responsible UKRep attachés; and the Minister's Private Secretary. The Minister's spouse or partner is also invited. Informals are a useful way to establish and develop working and personal relations between Ministers, diplomats and other officials. Despite the agreeable locations, real work gets done.

*Coreper*
All items which are to be considered by a Council have first to pass through the Committee of Permanent Representatives (or Coreper). The Committee is split into two, Coreper I and II, also known as Coreper (Deputies) and (Ambassadors). The Ambassadors or Permanent Representatives from each Representation sit on Coreper II, their Deputies (Deputy Permanent Representatives or DPRs) on Coreper I. Councils are shadowed by one or other Coreper:

**Coreper I:** Technical and internal Councils such as social affairs, health and environment.
**Coreper II:** Political and external Councils such as ECOFIN

(Economics and Finance Council) and the General Affairs Council

Coreper I usually meets on Wednesdays and Fridays and Coreper II on Thursdays, though this is arranged by the Presidency and must take account of other commitments of the Ambassadors, particularly Councils. They meet in Brussels or occasionally in Luxembourg, during the Council season. The Ambassador is assisted and briefed by attachés from the Permanent Representations: officials from Member State home civil services do not attend. As with the Council, Coreper sometimes meets in restricted session.

Two exceptions to the Coreper system are that: Agriculture Council business is prepared by the Special Committee on Agriculture (or SCA), while some ECOFIN business is prepared by the Economic Policy Committee or the Monetary Committee.

### Working Groups
*Dossiers* (matters for discussion, usually legislative proposals) are prepared for Coreper and Council by the Council working groups. There is one for each Council: Councils with a considerable amount of business have groups which meet two or more days each week, such as the Environment Working Group or the Social Questions Working Party. Others, such as the Civil Protection Working Group, meet so infrequently that they become half-forgotten. Timings and agendas for working groups are prepared by the Presidency and can vary at short notice, particularly in the run-up to a Council.

Each Member State is represented on the working groups by one or more attachés: as with meetings of the Council and Coreper, the Commission, Presidency and Council Secretariat are also present and can speak (though not vote). When appropriate, officials from the national administrations also participate. The proceedings of these working groups are confidential and only government officials may attend. The working groups are the main forum where UK officials negotiate and are dealt with in detail in Chapter 13.

**Reporting**

The proceedings of Council and Coreper are reported by UKRep on the same day (or night) by telegram to the Foreign Office, and are copied round Whitehall. Working groups are reported by UKRep by telegram to the FCO or (more commonly) by letter to the lead Whitehall department, then faxed and copied as appropriate. When officials from the UK attend, they usually produce more detailed notes on their individual subjects for a more limited circulation.

*Article 113 Committee*

The Commission has exclusive competence in the field of trade with third (non EU) countries under Article 113 of the Treaty. The Commission is advised on this issue by a committee of representatives of the Member States, known as the Article 113 Committee. DTI officials lead for the UK, with support from UKRep. Reporting is by telegram and letter. The Article 113 Committee also meets as what is, in effect, a sub-committee known as 'Article 113 (Deputies)'.

The Article 113 Committee is only consultative, advising the Commission on the views of the Member States on proposals concerning external trade, where the Commission runs the show (technically, has **exclusive competence**). As a result, it may have little impact on decisions taken in the Commission. Community competence is discussed in Chapter 8.

## The European Parliament

The 626 members of the European Parliament are directly elected every five years. The current Parliament was elected in 1994 and since the enlargement of the Union in 1995 has included 59 representatives from Austria, Finland and Sweden. Each Member State chooses its own means of election. Most use party lists: the UK alone has single-member constituencies and first-past-the-post elections (except for Northern Ireland's three MEPs, who are elected to a single constituency by proportional representation).

**Seats for each Country**

| | |
|---|---|
| Austria | 21 |
| Belgium | 25 |
| Denmark | 16 |
| Finland | 16 |
| France | 87 |
| Germany | 99 |
| Greece | 25 |
| Ireland | 15 |
| Italy | 87 |
| Luxembourg | 6 |
| Netherlands | 31 |
| Portugal | 25 |
| Spain | 64 |
| Sweden | 22 |
| United Kingdom | 87 |

The EP works more on political than on national lines: most MEPs represent national parties but sit in blocks with other (usually) like-minded parties from other Member States. The main parties, particularly the Socialist PSE and the Christian Democrat EPP, are well organised and fairly disciplined: some other groups exist largely to negotiate more effectively with the larger parties in dividing up the all-important posts chairing committees and reporting on legislative proposals. These looser groups include some bizarre political alliances.

**Political Groupings (1994–9)**

| | |
|---|---|
| Party of European Socialists (PSE) | 217 |
| European People's Party (EPP) | 173 |
| Union Group for Europe | 54 |
| European Liberal Democratic and Reformist Party | 52 |
| European United Left/Nordic Green Left | 33 |
| Greens | 27 |
| European Radical Alliance | 20 |

| Europe of Nations Group | 19 |
|---|---|
| Non-attached | 31 |
| | |
| Total | 626 |

The 62 UK Labour MEPs (known as the European Parliamentary Labour Party or EPLP) and the one Social Democratic and Labour Party MEP (John Hume) are members of the PSE; the 18 Conservatives MEPs are aligned less formally with the EPP, together with the one Ulster Unionist (James Nicholson); the two Liberal Democrats sit with the Liberal Democrat and Reformist group, and the two Scottish Nationalists (SNP) are part of the European Radical Alliance; the one Democratic Unionist MEP, Ian Paisley, is non-attached.

*The Role of the European Parliament*
The EP's role is to advise, scrutinise and, in certain circumstances, adopt legislation jointly with the Council. It is also, together with the Council, the budgetary authority of the Community and has the final say on 'non-compulsory' (crudely, non-agricultural) spending in the annual budget process.

*Committees*
As with many continental parliaments, the EP works through a system of committees covering each main area of policy. The number of MEPs on each committee varies; most MEPs sit on one or two at most; full members may also have stand-ins (*alternates*) who are entitled to attend, speak and vote in their place. Each committee has a chair and a number of vice-chairs who represent the main parties and together form the 'bureau', which manages the work of the committee, including the allocation of dossiers and timing of debates.

## The Permanent Committees of the European Parliament

Foreign Affairs, Security and Defence
Security and Disarmament
Human Rights
Agriculture and Rural Development
Budgets
Economic and Monetary Affairs and Industrial Policy
Monetary Affairs
Research, Technological Development and Energy
Social Affairs and Employment
Regional Policy
Transport and Tourism
Environment, Public Health and Consumer Protection
Culture, Youth, Education and the Media
Development and Co-operation
Civil Liberties and Internal Affairs
Budgetary Control
Institutional Affairs
Fisheries
Rules of Procedure, Credentials and Immunities
Women's Rights
Petitions

Typically, the committees meet every three weeks (though not in August), usually in Brussels, and their sittings are open to representatives from the Council, Member States, Commission and the public: of these, only the Commission may speak, when asked to explain proposals or answer other questions. The President of the Council is usually invited to address the relevant committee at the start of each Presidency and to answer questions from MEPs.

*The Legislative Processes of the Parliament*
The European Parliament contributes to almost all EU legislative acts by adopting Opinions: these start out as

reports from a single MEP (the *rapporteur*), amended and adopted first by the committee and then by the plenary.

The role of the rapporteur is a vital one: the dossiers are divided up between the political groupings, each group having a series of points according to their size with which they can 'bid' for proposals. Within political groupings, individual MEPs press for dossiers on the basis of their personal standing.

Once allocated – and rapporteurs may be appointed even before the Commission has formally adopted a proposal – the lucky MEP may draft his report on any basis he likes: some make considerable use of the Parliament's research unit or the functionaries who manage the business of the committees, and these officials often end up writing the first draft of the report; others use their own researchers; most at least discuss the proposal with the Commission and with representatives of outside groups; many are already fairly expert on the dossier and will write most of the report themselves.

However drafted, the report will (in the case of legislative proposals rather the Parliamentary initiatives such as Resolutions) include a series of proposed amendments to the proposal from the Commission (in the case of first readings) or to the Council's common position (in the case of second readings).

The draft report prepared by the rapporteur forms the basis for debate in the committee. The timing of debates – there may be more than one, particularly if the proposal is complicated, controversial or takes a long time to pass through the Council to a common position – is determined by the committee bureau. The rapporteur introduces his or her report, and other MEPs and the Commission comment on it. MEPs may also make their own points and table their own draft amendments between debates: the rapporteur and Commission will, in turn, comment on these amendments at the next opportunity.

Typically, the committee votes on the report and other draft amendments at its next sitting after the final debate. The chair of the committee will group together amendments on a single theme or political point, and also decide, where different proposed amendments cover the same point, which should be dropped when others are accepted. This gives the chair of the committee considerable power to impress his or her own views and personality on the committee.

Those amendments adopted by the committee go forward to the plenary sessions of the EP (held once every three or four weeks, usually in Strasbourg), to be voted on by all MEPs. Additional amendments may also be tabled at plenary by the political groups. Where a dossier has an impact on areas beyond the remit of the committee, other committees may produce an opinion of their own in roughly the same way. As in Westminster, the EP has business managers who negotiate amongst themselves to resolve differences of approach and try to ensure that a coherent set of amendments is tabled to plenary. Each group will also issue **voting lists** for plenary sessions, and also for many committee meetings, indicating which way to vote (for, against or abstain) on each amendment. Voting in committee and plenary can be very rapid (there may be over 100 amendments to a single proposal) and voting lists ensure MEPs do not vote the wrong way by accident.

*The Commission and the Parliament*
In the Community's legislative process, the roles of the Parliament and the Commission overlap. Once the Commission has formally transmitted its proposal to the Council and Parliament, Commission officials will give the committee an oral presentation of its main points (as it does in outline to the Council and in detail to the Council working group). It will also attend subsequent debates and answer any questions from MEPs. Commission officials, and sometimes even Commissioners themselves, will attend plenary sessions: Commissioners, as quasi-politicians, are well placed to engage in political debate and high-powered lobbying to help their position to pass through the plenary essentially intact.

The Commission frequently comments on proposed amendments before, during and after the Parliamentary stages of the legislative process. This is significant, since once a public position is taken, it is difficult for the Commission to back away from it. As Chapter 3 explains,

the position of the Commission on Parliamentary amendments can be crucial, as if the Commission supports them,
the Council has to act unanimously to reject them. The
Commission also plays an important role with the Parliament in the Conciliation Committee (see p. 58).

---

**The Moving Parliament**
The European Parliament plenary sessions are mainly
held in Strasbourg, but the central services are based in
Luxembourg and the MEPs' offices are in Brussels. The
EP therefore spends 10% or so of its budget moving
people and papers between the three locations. The
Parliament itself wishes to settle in Brussels, and has
new offices which include a suitable chamber, but the
Council has blocked this.

---

## The European Court of Justice

The ECJ is based in Luxembourg and consists of fifteen
judges and six advocate-generals appointed by consensus
(*common accord* is the term used in the Treaty) by the
Member States for terms of six years. It is the highest legal
authority in the Community and its decisions are binding on
Member States, companies and individuals. It deals with
two broad classes of actions: those referred to it by the
national courts of the Member States for rulings of interpretation of Community law (such cases then go back to
national courts); and those started before the ECJ by one or
other of the Community institutions (usually the Commission against the Member States).

The Court may consider a case in full or as a *chamber* of
three or five judges. First, the facts set out in the documents
and the oral pleadings are considered by an advocate-
general, whose formal written Opinion is usually (but not
always) followed by the full Court. Decisions by the Court
are always unanimous: dissenting Opinions by one or more
of the judges, as with the House of Lords, are not allowed.

Cases often take years to come before the ECJ, and months

can pass even between the Opinion of the advocate-general and the judgment of the Court itself. The Court can, nevertheless, move more quickly on occasions and is also able to grant injunctions. To relieve some of the burden, the Court of First Instance was set up to consider cases brought by staff employed by the Community institutions and certain cases brought under EU competition rules and the European Coal and Steel Community. Despite its name, it does not deal with cases on a preliminary basis.

Chapter 4 contains more details on the workings of the Community's legal system.

---

**Not the ECHR**
The media, followed by the general public, have endless difficulty distinguishing between the European Court of Justice (part of the Community and based in Luxembourg) and the European Court of Human Rights (set up by inter-governmental treaty under the auspices of the Council of Europe and based in Strasbourg). Unpopular decisions of the latter are often blamed on 'meddling Brussels loonycrats'.

Add in the International Court of Justice in the Hague and you have total confusion.

---

## Other Community Institutions and Agencies

*The Economic and Social Committee*
The ESC (also known as ECOSOC, which confusingly is the name of a separate UN committee) is an advisory body consisting of 220 representatives appointed by the Council every four years from industry, unions and other interest groups. The Treaty (Article 294) requires that the Committee be consulted on certain proposals: as with the EP, the ESC uses a system of sub-committees and rapporteurs to produce Opinions or Reports.

The importance of the ESC has declined in comparison to that of the European Parliament but it does still influence the legislative process. When planning to lobby the EP, the value of lobbying the ESC as well should be considered. ESC Reports and Opinions tend to have most impact when they are published early in the negotiating process and before those of the EP.

## Committee of the Regions
Established in 1994, its 220 members are appointed by the Member States, drawn from regional, local and munici-pal government. They have the right to be consulted on proposals covering health, education, youth, culture, eco-nomic and social cohesion and the Trans-European Net-works programme.

The Committee has the same structure of specialist committees and plenary sessions (five each year) and shares services with the Economic and Social Committee, but has now moved to the same Brussels site as the European Parliament.

## The Court of Auditors
This body, whose fifteen members are appointed by the Member States and assisted by 400 or so civil servants, examines the accounts of the EU and its institutions to assist the Council and the European Parliament in controlling the implementation of the budget. Also it may, at the request of the Council, EP or ECJ, or on its own initiative, report on a specific issue of proper management of Community resour-ces (those famous reports on Euro-waste).

## The Ombudsman
The Ombudsman is appointed by the European Parliament to investigate complaints of maladministration made by any citizen or body such as a company incorporated in the EU against any of the European institutions (except the ECJ). The institution and the complainant may comment on the Ombudsman's findings before a report is submitted to the Parliament. The Ombudsman also submits an annual report to the EP.

## Community Agencies
The Community has devolved various tasks to separate

agencies, most of which are based outside the Brussels–Luxembourg–Strasbourg axis. The work of most is self-evident from their titles:

European Centre for the Development of Vocational Training (CEDEFOP) (Thessaloniki)

European Foundation for the Improvement of Living and Working Conditions (Dublin)

European Environment Agency (Copenhagen)

European Agency for the Evaluation of Medical Products (EMEA) (London)

Office for Harmonisation in the Internal Market (OHIM) (Alicante): deals with registration of trademarks and designs

European Monitoring Centre for Drugs and Drug Addiction (Lisbon)

European Training Foundation (Turin)

Translation Centre for the European Institutions (Luxembourg)

European Agency for Health and Safety at Work (Bilbao)

Community Plant Variety Office (currently in Brussels)

EUROPOL (European Police Office) and EUROPOL Drugs Unit (the Hague)

European Statistics Office (EUROSTAT) (Luxembourg)

# Chapter 3
# The Legislative Process

*The UK Representation in Brussels is always ready to give expert tactical advice:*

*UKRep: Hello? . . . Yes? . . . That's right. So you want to adopt a Directive? . . . Hmm, yeah, all very difficult . . . Well, it's April, isn't it? Couldn't possibly let you have anything until the June Council at the earliest. Got your Opinion yet? . . . Oh dear, oh dear. Can't move without an Opinion from the European Parliament . . . Not my fault, mate. Love to help, but what can I do? More than my job's worth. You've got an Article 189b situation, haven't you? You've got your six weeks in Council, then your two months in the Commission. It's conciliation, see? Course, your legal base looks right up the spout. Have you thought about chopping this Directive in for something else? Got a lovely minutes statement in this week . . . Well, if you change your mind . . .*

## Introduction

In the good old days, adopting European legislation was simple: the Commission proposed legislation and the Council modified it in negotiation, taking account of the opinions of the European Parliament and the Economic and Social Committee. All very straightforward. Then, in the early 1980s, some bright spark thought, 'Let's give the Parliament more power.'

As a result, Community legislation now rarely follows a linear path from conception to adoption. There are three basic variations on the process, based around three different ways of bringing the European Parliament into the decision-making process. The choice of process is determined by the **legal base** of the proposal. The legal base also determines the method of **voting** for agreeing legislation: most legislation now uses a system of votes weighted to take account of the size of each Member State, known as **Qualified Majority Voting**. Each of these procedures has its own variations, so that the process now resembles the game of three-dimensional chess played on the Starship *Enterprise*.

The good news is that the process only becomes so complex after the **common position** has been reached: that is, after the Council has agreed what shape it thinks the proposal should take. Up to then, during the bulk of the negotiations, things are more simple. And most of the time, it is reaching the common position which is the most important part of the process.

## Legal Base

All Community acts have to be based on legal powers contained in one or more of the Articles of the Treaty: the *Legal Base* or *Treaty Base*. The choice of Article is determined, in theory, by the nature and primary aim of the proposal, so that, for example, a measure intended to harmonise standards for emissions from cars would have as its main aim harmonisation rather than environmental protection and would therefore be based on Article 100a (which deals with the internal market) rather than Article 130s (the environment).

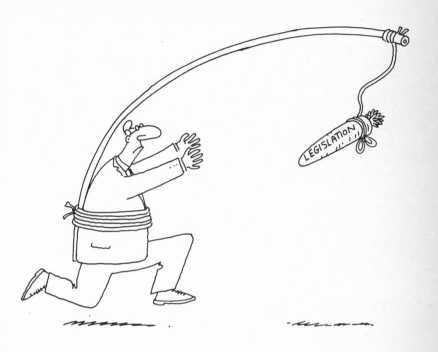

In practice, many proposals have more than one aim, and so political considerations come into play to determine the legal base and thus the arrangements for voting and for consulting the Parliament. The legal base put forward by the Commission as part of its draft proposal may be changed by the Council, in conjunction with the Parliament, under the same voting arrangements as for the proposal itself. In practice, the Council will usually need to agree to change it by unanimity. In the last resort, disputes about the legal base are settled by the European Court of Justice.

**Finding the Legal Base**
Community legislation must have a legal base in the Treaty: finding out what it is, however, can be tricky. Instinctively, people work through from the start of the Directive or Regulation. In fact, this key fact lurks in the recitals, before the main body of text. There will always be a recital phrased something like:

*Having regard to the Treaty, and in particular Article 100a [or whatever] thereof;*

This should save much flicking through the text and much muttering of 'Where the hell is it?'

## Voting

The procedure chosen also affects the mechanism for agreement within the Council. There are three variants:

- **Simple Majority**: more than half the Member States (8 out of 15) must vote for the proposal. Abstentions are therefore, in effect, votes against.
- **Qualified Majority (QMV)**: each Member State has a weighted vote (see box). There must be 62 votes for the proposal (although votes in the range 59–61 are covered by a special voting arrangement known as the **Ioannina Agreement** (see p. 64 below). Again, abstentions are, in effect, votes against.
- **Unanimity**: all voting Member States must support the measure. Abstentions are **not** therefore votes against.

**Voting Weights (Article 148)**

| | |
|---|---|
| Austria | 4 |
| Belgium | 5 |
| Denmark | 3 |
| France | 10 |
| Finland | 3 |
| Germany | 10 |

| | |
|---|---|
| Greece | 5 |
| Ireland | 3 |
| Italy | 10 |
| Luxembourg | 2 |
| Netherlands | 5 |
| Portugal | 5 |
| Spain | 8 |
| Sweden | 4 |
| United Kingdom | 10 |
| Total | 87 |

A qualified majority requires 62* votes in favour
A blocking minority requires 26* votes against or abstentions

* but see the Ioannina Agreement (p. 64)

# Forms of Legislation

The Community has a range of legislative instruments (Regulations, Directives, Decisions) at its disposal (set out in Article 189), as well as other, non-binding instruments (Recommendations, Opinions). The Council also has its own forms of non-binding political statement. Each type of instrument has different effects and different rules governing its creation and adoption.

*Regulations*
A Regulation has general application and is binding in its entirety and directly applicable in all Member States. In other words, once a Regulation enters into force it forms part of the law of each Member State. Regulations may be adopted by the Council or jointly by the Council and the European Parliament: these are usually known simply as Regulations (or sometimes Council Regulations). The Council and the Treaty may also delegate powers to the Commission to adopt Regulations in specific policy areas (such as the detail of import controls or setting of sheep-meat prices), and these also are generally and directly applicable in all

Member States. They are usually termed Commission Regulations to avoid confusion with the parent (Council) Regulations.

## Directives

A Directive is binding on the Member States to which it is addressed as to the result to be achieved, but it is up to national authorities to choose the form and methods by which that result is secured. Directives therefore have to be *transposed* into national law (see Chapter 4) by means of national primary or secondary legislation. In the UK, this would be by Act of Parliament or, where Parliament has already passed an Act devolving powers to Ministers, by means of secondary measures such as Statutory Instruments or Orders in Council. As with Regulations, Directives can be adopted by the Council; the Council and the Parliament; or the Commission (within powers delegated by the Council or the Treaty).

## Decisions

A Decision is binding in its entirety upon those to whom it is addressed, whether individuals, companies or Member States, or the Community's own institutions. One example is the series of Commission Decisions on licences to trade ozone-depleting substances, which draw their legal basis from powers delegated by various Council Regulations to a Commission-chaired committee.

## Recommendations

These are non-binding instruments which have moral as opposed to legal force. As with other legislative acts, they are proposed by the Commission and pass through the Council and Parliament according to the Article of the Treaty on which the proposal is based. Recommendations set out the Community's view of necessary actions or procedures.

## Opinions

Opinions are also non-binding and work in a way very similar to Recommendations. The main difference is that they provide scope for views to be expressed without necessarily providing recommended courses of action.

## The First Phase – Reaching the Common Position

The legislative process usually starts with the expectation that the Community should act in a particular policy area. Pressure for this can come from any number of directions: public opinion, perhaps directed by individual incidents or campaigning groups; sectional interests; research on risks and hazards; technical or economic developments requiring new co-ordination or regulation; even pressure from individual Member States. What is rare is for the faceless Commission bureaucrat of lore to hatch up the idea of a Directive on, say, mushroom standards without some outside prompting.

Most Community action stems from external pressure:

**The Seals Directive**
Campaigning groups, in particular Greenpeace, raised public concern about the methods used by seal-hunters in Canada and elsewhere. The concern was taken up by the European Parliament in 1979 and by some Member States. Pressure was put on the Commission to propose an import ban on the skins of seal pups, which was agreed by the Council in 1981.

**The Seveso Directive**
In 1976, a fire at a chemical factory contaminated the town of Seveso in Italy with highly toxic dioxins. This, and other similar, if less well-known, incidents, prompted a Directive on the Control of Major Accident Hazards (still known as 'the Seveso Directive').

**The Lifts Directive**
As part of the single market (*Project 1992*), lift manufacturers wanted safety standards harmonised, so that the same product range could be sold throughout the

> Community. (They were a little surprised, though,
> when they found that the Directive also covered
> builders' hoists.)

Influences such as these build up pressure for action, which
might find expression in the Commission's non-binding
action programmes or be discussed at meetings between the
Commission and the relevant Directors-General from the
administrations of the Member States. Such informal sound-
ings and discussions help the Commission to sketch out the
possible shape of a proposal, and also to see how much
support – or otherwise – there would be. A Commissioner
would usually avoid risking credibility by pushing for
action in the face of insurmountable opposition.

The first formal response would be the inclusion of the
subject in the Commission's **annual work programme**.
Responsibility within the Commission services for originat-
ing a draft proposal for services would by then be assigned
to a specific unit or individual official. A **Commission
expert group** made up of the lead policy officials from each
Member State is usually convened to help the Commission
officials to formulate a proposal. It is chaired and serviced
by the Commission and may include representatives of
outside bodies such as industry. Such groups are discussed
in more detail in Chapters 5 and 13.

Once drafted, the proposal goes out from the parent
Directorate-General to the other DGs: the process known as
**inter-service consultation**. It also passes through the cabinets and may be altered at both stages to take account of the
wider views of the Commission. This provides an opportunity for lobbying Commission officials in the cabinets and in
other Directorates-General. Explaining your position or
providing further information can bring about significant
changes or helpful delays (see Chapter 14). Once finalised,
the proposal is put to the Commissioners for adoption. If
agreement amongst cabinet officials is not possible, the
proposal may be discussed by the Commissioners themselves.

Where the College of Commissioners cannot agree on a
proposal by consensus, it may vote on a proposal by a

simple majority of those Commissioners present. However, the tendency is to avoid such divisive votes and work for a compromise. Here, the role of the President (and his or her cabinet) is crucial.

Once the proposal has been adopted formally by the Commission, the text is sent to the Council Secretariat. This stage is followed (often some weeks later) by publication in the *Official Journal of the European Union* (the *OJ*). After publication, national administrations often begin formal consultation, notably of regional government and national Parliaments: the UK government, for example, presents the proposal to the UK Parliament for scrutiny, together with an Explanatory Memorandum prepared by the lead Whitehall department. (Supplementary Memoranda may be prepared as necessary at later stages of the UK Parliamentary scrutiny process.)

The Commission presents new proposals to the Council (at the next meeting of the relevant Council: there is usually no debate, though Member States may pass comment) and the Parliament (see p. 38). The proposal will then be taken up by a Presidency (not necessarily at once) and discussed in a **working group** of the Council (chaired by the Presidency and serviced by the Council Secretariat). As Chapter 2 explained, the working group tries to secure agreement on as much of the proposal as possible before it is forwarded to Coreper and the Council. Each working group has its own working methods, but usually each Member State is represented by an attaché from the Permanent Representation, briefed and assisted as necessary by experts from capitals.

In the Council, the Presidency has effective control of the legislative timetable. Proposals can languish for years if successive Presidencies give them a low priority.

**Coreper** (the Committee of Permanent Representatives) reviews the agreements reached in the working group and attempts to resolve outstanding points before the proposal is forwarded to the Council.

The **Council** then tries to reach a common position on a proposal, taking into account the Opinion of the European Parliament, as determined by the EP's *first reading* of the proposal. (For more on the Parliament's role in the legislative process, see Chapter 2.) The Council also takes note of the Opinion of the Economic and Social Committee and, for certain subjects, the Opinion of the Committee of the Regions. If a common position cannot be reached, the proposal is usually sent back to the working group, to return to a later Council via Coreper. The Presidency can also convene a **parallel working group** of officials while the Council is in session to try to resolve outstanding technical or drafting points, so allowing the measure to be agreed without delay.

Often, dossiers take many months to negotiate and the Presidency may ask the Council to take note of the progress made (known as a *progress report*) or to debate the overall shape the proposal should take (an *orientation debate*). In either case, a paper is prepared by the Presidency and Council Secretariat, negotiated in the working group and Coreper, and then discussed in Council.

*Formal Adoption of the Common Position*
The formal adoption of a common position can only take place when the Council has received the Opinion of the European Parliament. However, the Council is able to reach a **political agreement** towards a common position. In practice, there is little difference between the two except that the Council will need to confirm its political agreement as a common position at a later Council meeting. In either case, there are various technical but significant stages to go through before the exact text of the common position can be adopted.

*The Recitals*
First, the Council Secretariat will redraft the **recitals** (the preambular paragraphs or 'whereas' clauses) in the Commission proposal in the light of the shape of the modified text. This is then agreed by consensus in the working group. If agreement there is not possible, the text would pass to Coreper and (in theory) could go on to Council itself to be

voted on according to the voting arrangements for the proposal as a whole.

The recitals are important, as the ECJ will take them into account in construing the intentions of Council should doubt arise as to the meaning of specific provisions in the Articles of the text. The recitals should, on the one hand, merely reflect the provisions of the text agreed in the text in the Council, but they may also take account of political understandings or aspirations which could not, for whatever reason, be contained in the Articles. These two considerations are self-evidently incompatible, which can make negotiations over the recitals rather awkward.

## Jurist-Linguists

The text of both the Articles and the recitals passes to the **jurist-linguists** (or legal-linguists), a group made up of the Council Secretariat, the Council Legal Service and representatives of the Commission and of those Member States who choose to attend. The intention is to review the text to ensure they are properly and legally drafted and equivalent in all Community languages. There is scope for significant changes to the meaning of the proposal even at this stage, and officials from the Permanent Representations or even home departments attend many such meetings.

---

When jurist-linguists met in 1985 to consider the draft Environmental Impact Assessment Directive, a key point was whether Ministers had meant it to cover *salmon* (i.e., salmon) or *salmonids* (i.e., the salmon family, including trout and so trout farms). Getting such details right remains a major challenge but saves heartache over ambiguities when the legislation has to be transposed nationally.

---

The text agreed by the jurist-linguists then goes through Coreper and is adopted formally by Council as an 'A-Point' and so not necessarily by the Council which agreed the common position. In Whitehall, the lead department coordinates the clearance of A-Points and checks that the document containing the text is accurate: there is no chance for subsequent amendment. The common position, in this final form, is then sent to the European Parliament and Commission.

After a common position has been agreed, a second round with the Parliament takes place before the text is finalised and **adopted** as Community law. It is here that the three procedures go their separate ways.

## The Second Phase: From Common Position to Final Adoption

For those taking part in a negotiation, the moment that a common position is reached is one to savour. The deal is done, the Council bursts into applause, backs are slapped. But in the cold grey light of the following day comes the hangover: ensuring that the European Parliament and the Commission are fully consulted on the shape of this settlement without the whole agreement coming apart.

The three main variations which apply after common position are known as:

● Consultation
● Co-operation (Article 189c)
● Co-decision (Article 189b)

Consultation is the original procedure and is not described in a separate Article of the Treaty, while co-operation and co-decision are set out in Article 189. As explained above, the choice of procedure depends on the legal base of the proposal: the Commission includes the legal base in its proposal and the Council can change it using the same procedures as for the proposal as a whole.

The Commission and Council may agree some measures with little or no consultation of the Parliament. These are mainly commercial and trade agreements made under Article 113 (see Chapter 2), to which the procedures for consultation and adoption set out in Article 228 apply.

*Consultation*
This is the most straightforward procedure. The Parliament

produces only one Opinion and the Council is not obliged to modify its position in proceeding to final adoption of the legislation. Various Articles of the Treaty set out this procedure, including Article 228 (international agreements) and Article 235 (which allows the Community to act where no specific Treaty provisions apply). It is important to look closely at the detail of each Treaty Article which makes use of the consultation procedure: they are not always the same, as a brief comparison of these two Articles shows.

*Co-operation (Article 189c)*
Under this procedure, the common position is transmitted to the European Parliament, which has three months in which to complete its **second reading** (that is, its second Opinion on the proposal, this time as amended to form the Council's common position) and choose one of four options. These are:

(i) to take no decision
(ii) to approve the common position
(iii) to propose amendments to the common position (adopted by an absolute majority of MEPs, not a majority of those voting)
(iv) to reject the common position outright (again, by an absolute majority)

In practice, the EP imposes on itself the rule that amendments cannot be raised at second reading which were not part of the Opinion from the first reading. This rule, though, can be interpreted flexibly: for example, the EP will not necessarily bind itself if the common position reached by the Council includes provisions which differ markedly from those in the original Commission proposal (which is the document on which the EP gives its first Opinion).

The outcome of the second reading is transmitted to the Council and the Commission. **Options (i)** and **(ii)** lead to the Council adopting the common position as it stands. **Option (iv)** means that the Council can only adopt the common position by unanimity, even if the common position was originally reached by means of a qualified majority. The

Council may not, at this stage, change its proposal, even by unanimity.

**Option (iii)** is more complicated. The Commission has one month to re-examine the common position, taking into account the Parliament's proposed amendments. At the same time, it forwards to the Council its opinion of the Parliament's amendments which it has *not* incorporated into its re-examined proposal. Once it receives the Commission's re-examined proposal, the Council must then within three months either:

(i) do nothing (in which case the entire process ends without anything being adopted)
(ii) adopt the re-examined proposal from the Commission by **by Qualified Majority Voting**
(iii) amend the re-examined proposal (and this includes adopting the original common position) **by unanimity**

The view that the Commission takes on the amendments put forward by the Parliament is crucial: the Council may approve the amendments supported by the Commission by qualified majority, but may only approve amendments on which the Commission has given a negative opinion or reject amendments adopted by the Commission by unanimity.

> Remember that the co-operation procedure allows just one Member State, working with the Parliament and the Commission, to overturn a common position agreed by the Council by a qualified majority.

*Co-decision (Article 189b)*
Under the co-decision procedure, introduced in 1993 by the Maastricht Treaty, the views of the European Parliament cannot be set aside by the Council, even acting by unanimity: the Parliament has, in effect, the right to veto legislation. (The procedure is fairly complicated, and is also set out in a flowchart opposite.)

Once the common position has been agreed, it is sent to

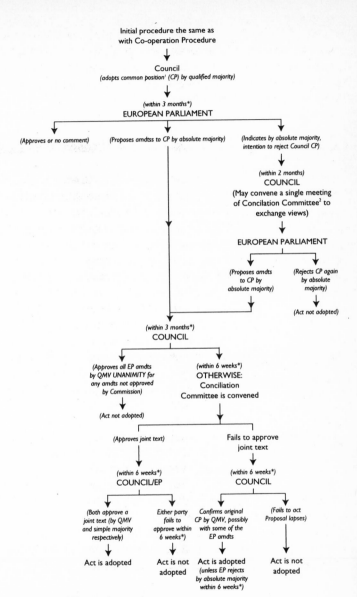

Initial procedure the same as
with Co-operation Procedure

↓

Council
*(adopts common position¹ (CP) by qualified majority)*

↓

*(within 3 months*)*
EUROPEAN PARLIAMENT

*(Approves or no comment)*          *(Proposes amdtss to CP by absolute majority)*          *(Indicates by absolute majority, intention to reject Council CP)*

*(within 2 months)*
COUNCIL
(May convene a single meeting
of Concilation Committee² to
exchange views)

↓

EUROPEAN PARLIAMENT

*(Proposes amdts
to CP by
absolute majority)*          *(Rejects CP again
by absolute
majority)*

*(Act not adopted)*

*(within 3 months*)*
COUNCIL

*(Approves all EP amdts
by QMV UNANIMITY for
any amdts not approved
by Commission)*          *(within 6 weeks*)*
OTHERWISE:
Conciliation
Committee is convened

*(Act not adopted)*

*(Approves joint text)*          Fails to approve
joint text

*(within 6 weeks*)*
COUNCIL/EP          *(within 6 weeks*)*
COUNCIL

*(Both approve a
joint text (by QMV
and simple majority
respectively)*          *Either party
fails to
approve within
6 weeks*)*          *Confirms original
CP by QMV, possibly
with some of the
EP amdts*          *(Fails to act
Proposal lapses)*

Act is adopted          Act is not
adopted          Act is adopted
*(unless EP rejects
by absolute majority
within 6 weeks*)*          Act is not
adopted

* These periods can be extended by one month or two weeks.
¹ At this and all subsequent stages, the Council acts by unanimity in some fields, eg Research,
² Conciliation Committee comprises 15 representatives each from Council and EP. Council acts by QMV. EP acts by majority.
ARTICLES AFFECTED BY THE CODECISION PROCEDURE
The procedure begins when the Commision puts forward a proposal to the Council under one of the following Articles of the Treaty of Rome as amended
by the Maastrict Treaty ie. Articles 49, 54(2), 56(2), 57(1), 57(2), 66, 100a(1), 100b, 126(4), 128(5), 129(4), 129a(2), 129d, 130t(1); and 130s(3).

the Parliament and to the Commission, which in turn informs the Parliament of its position on the proposal. The Parliament then has three months to respond. Its options are:

(i) to do **nothing**, in which case the Council adopts the common position unchanged

(ii) to **approve** the common position, in which case the Council adopts it unchanged

(iii) to **reject** the common position by an absolute majority of MEPs (after giving the Council an opportunity to explain further its position), in which case the proposal is lost

(iv) to propose **amendments** to the common position by an absolute majority of MEPs. These amendments are then passed to the Council and also to the Commission, which delivers an opinion on them. If the Council is unable to adopt all the amendments proposed by the Parliament, the **conciliation committee** must be convened.

The Council has three months after the proposal returns to it in which to try to adopt the proposal, and the view that the Commission takes on the amendments put forward by the Parliament is crucial: the Council may approve by qualified majority the amendments supported by the Commission, **but may only approve by unanimity amendments on which the Commission has given a negative opinion**.

If, as a result of these constraints, the Council is unable to adopt all the amendments proposed by the Parliament, the Conciliation Committee must be convened.

*The Conciliation Committee*
The role of the Committee is to prepare a joint text for approval by the Council (by qualified majority) and the Parliament (by a majority of MEPs). The Committee consists of representatives from the Council (effectively Coreper) and from the Parliament (a group of up to fifteen MEPs, not necessarily from the relevant EP committee!), co-chaired by the leader of the Parliament's delegation and by the Presidency of the Council (sometimes by a Minister from the Presidency, supported by his or her country's Ambassador or Deputy Ambassador). It is serviced by both the Parliament and Council Secretariats and meets either in the

Parliament or Council building.

The Conciliation Committee is a strange body. Ranged on one side are MEPs and their assistants: they tend to focus on the political aspects, as only the rapporteur and a handful of others actually know the detail of the proposal. Against them are ranged the fifteen Ambassadors or Deputies, who are supposed to leave the Presidency to speak for them to an agreed position and are not well placed to respond to the cut and thrust of political debate which the politicians from the Parliament bring to the meeting.

A Committee meeting may be pre-cooked in exchanges between the Presidency and Parliament, often with the Commission acting as an intermediary ('honest broker' would be going too far, as the Commission has its own positions to defend). If such an informal agreement cannot be reached, the Conciliation Committee would negotiate on the substance, each side having pre-meetings to establish positions and fall-backs.

Over its short life the Committee has been unpredictable both in its final product and in the way it has conducted itself. It convenes, breaks for consultations, returns, breaks again, all conducted in a flurry of whispered exchanges and wild rumours outside the meeting room, and posturing and sarcasm within. But from this unlikely mélange, agreement can flow.

Assuming a text is produced, the Council and the Parliament must adopt the legislation within six weeks (extendable to eight weeks by the agreement of both parties). It is not likely that the Council would fail to act within this time, as it can adopt the text as an A-Point at any Council meeting. However, the assent of the European Parliament is less certain: there is a greater chance that the EP would reject the deal brokered by its representatives, and also the Parliament must adopt the text at a plenary session by an absolute majority of MEPs. (Given some attendance records, there can be no guarantee that enough MEPs will turn up to support a measure, particularly at the poorly attended December plenary session.)

**If either Council or Parliament does not adopt the proposal within the deadline, it is lost.**

If the Conciliation Committee fails to agree a text, the

Council may, by a qualified majority, adopt its common position either as it stands or with amendments suggested by the Parliament. The Parliament may then reject the proposal, by an absolute majority of MEPs, within six weeks. If it does so, the proposal is lost. If it does not, the proposal is adopted.

---

**Deadlines**
The procedures under Article 189(b) and (c) make great use of deadlines, and as proposals can pass or fall on a matter of a few days, the exact point that these start and end can be vital. In essence, it is from the date of official transmission (for example, when the Secretary-General of the Commission writes to the Council to transmit a proposal formally). In the case of the European Parliament, however, the deadlines start from the date of the first plenary session following formal receipt of a proposal or other document. All these rules can be interpreted fluidly, so it is best to check in all cases where the exact deadline matters.

---

## Other Council Procedures – Policy Statements

The Council may also advance policy formation through other non-binding means: Council Conclusions, Council Resolutions, and Statements in the Council Minutes. These do not need to be based on Commission proposals nor does the European Parliament need to be consulted. The choice between using Conclusions and Resolutions is made by the Presidency, based on tradition and the nature of the subject matter.

*Council Conclusions*
Conclusions are statements of the policy intentions of the Council and may include programmes for future work. Conclusions are also used where a Council does not wish to, or cannot, take legislative action. The texts of Conclusions

are usually brokered in working group and Coreper before going to Council, where they can only be adopted by unanimity.

*Council Resolutions*
These are similar to Conclusions, but have more the flavour of a political (though not legal) commitment to a specified course of action. In other words, Conclusions might say, 'X is a real problem, and we, the Council or the Member States, should do something', while Resolutions might say, 'X is a real problem, and we, the Council or the Member States, should therefore do Y.' Resolutions are dealt with in the same way as Conclusions.

*Council Minutes Statements*
The Commission and any Member State may enter a statement in the minutes of the Council. These statements are usually confidential, unless the proponent decides otherwise. However, the Council Rules of Procedure have recently been revised to increase openness and transparency (the jury is still out on the effectiveness of this).

---

There are three broad types of minutes statement:

● **Informative**: where one or more Member States or the Commission wish to record a matter of fact.
● **Political**: this allows Member States to make public or confidential statements on their attitude to Council acts and other policy areas. Statements that one or more Member States intend to take further action beyond the terms of a Directive or Regulation are quite common.
● **Interpretative**: these interpret or gloss the meaning of legislation. They have been outlawed by the Council Legal Service and the ECJ has ruled that such interpretative statements have no legal force: that is, cannot be used in Court proceedings. Nevertheless, old statements of this type linger in the minutes. Also, some may still creep in as they are useful in securing agreements and can additionally have the force of a political or moral commitment. As an example, if the Commission entered a statement in the minutes to the

effect that a Member State could interpret a Directive in a particular way, it would then be very unlikely that the Commission would renege on that statement and pursue that Member State through the infractions system over that interpretation. (Unlikely, but not impossible: the Commission sometimes argues that it is not bound by such deals done by preceding Colleges of Commissioners.)

As a matter of principle, and for the sake of legal certainty, the use of minutes statements is avoided as far as possible: better that the text of the Regulation or Directive itself be drafted clearly and unambiguously. Where this is not possible, minutes statements come into play. They are not voted on, though if all Member States can support a statement it clearly has more moral (though not legal) force. Minutes statements cannot be blocked, though others can enter minutes statements of their own to dispute an assertion or policy line.

*Council Rules of Procedure*
The Council adopts its own Rules of Procedure. These are well worth looking at for officials attending Council meetings. Most are self-explanatory; a few need further explanation. Generally, the most significant rules are probably those concerning the Council agenda.

*Council Agendas*
All Member States have the right to add items to the agenda of a Council meeting and to insist that a vote is taken. Such items must be added formally by the Member State at least fifteen days before the Council is due to meet. It is only by the agreement of all Member States that items can be added afterwards and voted upon.

In practice, the agenda is drawn up by the Presidency, so that a Member State which attempts to force a debate against the wishes of the Presidency and other Member States is likely to come off badly. The essential step is to build up support amongst other Member States for adding the item to the agenda (after consulting UKRep) well in advance of the Council.

## A-Points
The agenda will contain two lists: A- and B-Points (or items). A-Points are those which are uncontroversial and which need no discussion: most will be those usually dealt with by another Council (and so can be anything from workers' rights to fish quotas). If any Member State cannot adopt an A-Point, that item must be dropped. Dropped items can be reinstated on the list of B-Points, but note that such items would then be added fewer than fifteen days before the Council, allowing a Member State to block a vote on the matter (if it chose to take the criticism for doing so: most Council business is based on a spirit of co-operation rather than rigid adherence to the rules of procedure, and quoting rules can lead to others being quoted back at the worst possible times!).

## B-Points
The list of B-Points covers those items which are subject to debate by Ministers. In the Agriculture Council, for example, these would all be agricultural dossiers. Those points which may be put to the vote are usually marked with an asterisk (and so known as *starred B-Points*). To help avoid too strict a distinction between A-points and B-points, there is a system of *false B-Points* where one or more Member States makes a statement into the Council minutes about a proposal (which, like A-Points, can be on any subject for any Council). Once the statement has been made, the proposal is adopted without further discussion. Any further discussion, let alone a vote, would not be possible.

## Items of Other Business
AOB (any other business) items follow the B-Points. Member States can add as many items as they wish; however, as no other Member State need reply to presentations, the usefulness of AOB items can be overstated. It is expected that the Member State adding an item should circulate an explanatory note through the Council Secretariat well in advance of the Council meeting, setting out the issue. As

with all other proposals, prior preparation is needed with the Presidency, Commission and other Member States.

## Lunch

The Presidency will arrange for some items to be discussed during lunch, when Ministers eat separately from officials (which gives the opportunity for policy traps or *bounces*). No item can be voted on or decided over lunch, but some subjects may return to the formal Council session for further discussion or even a decision.

## The Luxembourg Compromise

Where decisions subject to qualified majority voting concern very important interests for one or more Member States, the Council has an informal agreement to try to find a solution which can be agreed by unanimity: this is the Luxembourg Compromise. It is not, as sometimes suggested, a power of veto: the original Compromise of 1966 and the later modification of 1974 instead allow for endeavours to reach compromises under exceptional circumstances. Also, the Council may override the Compromise (as happened to the UK during the Community budget negotiations in 1982).

The Luxembourg Compromise is **extremely sensitive**, and Whitehall has an elaborate procedure for consideration and consultation which applies in all cases where it may be used by the UK or any other Member State. Its possible use is never threatened or even hinted at by the UK in negotiations, except after this process.

## Ioannina Agreement

In 1994, the accession of Finland, Sweden and Austria to the Union led to changes in the system of Qualified Majority Voting. The *blocking minority* was raised from 23 votes to 26 votes; this was balanced by an agreement amongst Member States to the effect that, where a minority opposed to a proposal had between 23 and 25 votes, they could request that the vote be delayed to allow for further efforts to reach a compromise which more Member States could support. This Ioannina Agreement was also intended to influence Presidencies when they consider whether to push a controversial measure to a vote or to work on for a compromise.

The Agreement and the conditions under which it might be invoked have a particular political sensitivity.

# Chapter 4
# Community Law

### The Administrators' Nightmare (I)

*A faceless modern Brussels office block, all glass and steel. Deep in its heart, far underground, rows of operators stare grimly into computer screens or move counters over a map of Britain set out on a huge plotting table. High above, a hatchet-faced official surveys the scene, then snarls into a microphone.*

*'Move our forces into the Western sector! The targets are Twyford Down, Oxleas Wood, the Medway Estuary . . .'*

*As the list goes on, salvoes of Article 169 letters are launched towards an unsuspecting Whitehall.*

## Introduction

In fact, the Commission is no all-powerful, omniscient colossus. The resemblance to the world of *Dr Strangelove* or *The Man from UNCLE* is to be seen only in the dated sixties furniture and décor of its offices. There is no master plan. The Commission acts more in response to outside pressures, scanty resources or its own ignorance than any sinister design.

The Commission does, however, have a job to do: to oversee the implementation and enforcement of Community law. To this end, Member States have a duty to **transpose** Community legislation fully and on time; to **notify** the Commission of this transposition; and to **implement** and enforce the legislation properly. The final obligation on Member States is to co-operate in any proper enquiry the Commission may undertake to ensure that these duties have been carried out and that there has been no breach or **infraction** of Community law. In Britain, the lead Whitehall department is responsible for ensuring that the duties in each Directive or Regulation are fulfilled, while the Cabinet Office, backed by the FCO and UKRep, leads on the wider policy of European law.

One point to clarify: the terms *transposition* and *implementation* are used throughout this guide as above. However, in Whitehall, and even in the Commission, they are often confused, particularly by using *implementation* to cover the whole process from transposition to enforcement.

## Transposition

Council and Commission Regulations are *directly applicable* in the Member States: that is, a Member State does not need to enact any further legal measures for them to have legal force, although some 'top-up' measures such as penalties may be needed. Indeed, duplicating the provisions of the Regulation in domestic legislation would not normally be allowed, and pre-existing measures that are incompatible with the Regulation would need to be repealed to ensure that the *legal certainty* necessary for the proper operation of the Regulation is not put in doubt.

Council and Commission Directives must be transposed into national law. This may be achieved solely through primary legislation; or through secondary legislation (such as Statutory Instruments) using the powers in section 2(2) of the European Communities Act 1972 or other more specific powers in primary legislation; or by means of Directions (provided certain conditions are met); or a combination of these. The use of administrative means (such as circulars or guidance notes) is not a proper form of transposition.

Community acts have a date at which they *enter into force*: crudely, when they come on to the statute book. They may also have one or more dates at which some or all of the specific provisions of the legislation *come into effect*. Acts enter into force either on the twentieth day after they are published in the *Official Journal* (Article 191) or on the date specified in the text of the legislation (almost always the latter). Provisions come into effect on the date of entry into force unless other dates are specified in the text. Taken together, these dates create one or more deadlines by which transposition must be completed.

## Deadlines

In negotiations, the realism of the deadlines proposed by the Commission need to be considered by government and by those affected by the measures. The usual deadline is two years from the date of adoption to the date of entry into force, which may not be long enough for transposition to be completed in Scotland, Northern Ireland and Gibraltar (see p. 128), particularly if primary legislation is required. There must also be policy judgements about the realism of the timing of the specific provisions.

Some provisions in Directives create rights and obligations which are precise and unconditional and which, even if not transposed into national law, may have *direct effect*. This means that the rights and obligations exist in national law even though the necessary transposing legislation has not, for whatever reason, been adopted. This does not cancel out the need for the Directive to be transposed (it does not turn a Directive into a Regulation) but does allow for legal challenge against a Member State government (or any 'emanation' of the State, such as a health authority). Further, even if the provisions do not have direct effect, they may nevertheless create a right of compensation (following the ECJ judgment on the *Francovich* case). Fortunately, this whole murky area can be avoided by transposing fully and on time.

Sometimes, the implementation of a Directive may be

combined with supplementary, purely domestic measures. It is critical to distinguish, for Ministers and for the outside world, which is which: where measures are the result of domestic decisions, and where they can honestly be attributed to requirements from the EU. Where the scope of the requirements imposed by a Directive is unclear, the matter is always referred to Ministers to decide.

## Notification of Transposition to the Commission

All national measures necessary to transpose Community legislation must be notified to the Commission by the date of entry into force unless the text of the Directive states otherwise. Notification is by letter from UKRep to the Secretary-General of the Commission (copied to the Director-General of the DG responsible for the legislation), enclosing copies of all the transposing measures. It is the duty of each government department to ensure that this happens by supplying UKRep with a draft letter, although the Cabinet Office does monitor transposition.

The draft letter usually states whether Scotland, Northern Ireland and Gibraltar are covered by the legislation to avoid the Commission starting the infraction process automatically and without any further warning for these territories. If transposition does not cover these territories this would normally be made clear in the letter to the Commission and an explanation and a target date for full transposition offered. The obligation to notify also includes updates or amendments to domestic legislation, including legislation which has been amended to take account of an infraction case.

The Commission often sends a letter of reminder to all Member States a few months before the due date for transposition of a Directive into national law. Such letters occasionally refer to 'transposition tables' or raise points about the means of transposition, and when a reply is requested are therefore treated in the same way as pre-Article 169 letters (see p. 77 below).

If legislation is not **transposed** in its totality by the due date, this is a breach of Community law and can also cause *legal uncertainty* for businesses and individuals, which may give rise to domestic legal actions and claims for compensation against the Government. If such a position arises, perhaps because of unexpected difficulties with transposing legislation in the UK Parliament, it is usual to send some sort of explanation to the Commission (including some idea when transposition will take place) with a view to staving off an infraction case.

---

**Timely Transposition**
Even a few days makes a difference: the greatest number of UK infraction cases on a single point of law concern a Directive which was transposed just *twelve days* late. Some of these cases were still not settled ten years after the date the Directive entered into force.

---

If Community legislation has not been **notified** by the due date, the Commission will automatically start infraction proceedings (this really is automatic: the Secretariat-General of the Commission has a large computer which produces the papers without prompting). If the legislation has been transposed, the proceedings are clearly an unnecessary waste of time. The infraction case will also count against the record on proper and timely implementation of the Member State concerned. All amendments to transposing legislation must also be notified to the Commission in the same way.

## Implementation

The European Communities Act 1972 in effect makes Community law the law of the land. Under section 2(1), all rights which under Community law are to be recognised by national courts (such as Regulations and Decisions) are automatically part of national law; section 2(2) provides for other Community acts to be transposed into national legislation by regulations. Therefore Community law should never be seen as 'soft law' and its obligations must be taken as seriously as those in purely domestic legislation such as Acts of Parliament or Statutory Instruments.

**Section 2 of the European Communities Act 1972**
**General implementation of Treaties**
2—(1) All such rights, powers, liabilities, obligations and restrictions from time to time created or arising by or under the Treaties, and all such remedies and procedures from time to time provided for by or under the Treaties, as in accordance with the Treaties are without further enactment to be given legal effect or used in the United Kingdom shall be recognised and available in law, and be enforced, allowed and followed accordingly; and the expression 'enforceable Community right' and similar expressions shall be read as referring to one to which this subsection applies.

(2) Subject to Schedule 2 to this Act, at any time after its passing Her Majesty may by Order in Council, and any designated Minister or department may by regulations, make provision –

*(a)* for the purpose of implementing any Community obligation of the United Kingdom, or enabling any such obligation to be implemented, or of enabling any rights enjoyed or to be enjoyed by the United Kingdom under or by virtue of the Treaties to be exercised; or *(b)* for the purpose of dealing with matters arising out of or related to any such obligation or rights or the coming into force, or the operation from time to time, of subsection (1) above;

and in the exercise of any statutory power or duty, including any power to give directions or to legislate by means of orders, rules, regulations or other subordinate instrument, the person entrusted with the power or duty may have regard to the objects of the Communities and to any such obligation or rights as aforesaid.

In this subsection 'designated Minister or department' means such Minister of the Crown or government department as may from time to time be designated by Order in Council in relation to any matter or for any purpose, but subject to such restrictions or conditions (if any) as may be specified by the Order in Council.

## Infractions of Community Law

Those who have gone to law in Britain, whether for high treason or over a faulty lawnmower, will probably already have learnt the hard way some simple but crucial lessons about the legal process: it is **expensive, time-consuming** and **unpredictable**.

In the case of infractions, the **expense** is in the cost of remedial works, the damaging negative publicity, and the fees for barristers; the **time** includes the resources and effort on the part of officials, which could be better invested in the everyday task of running Britain; and the **unpredictability** covers not only the decision of the Court on the immediate points of law at issue, but also the wider implications of whatever they might decide. And if the final judgment is not implemented in full by the Member State concerned, the whole case can return to the ECJ, which may then impose a fine.

The smart thing, therefore, is to avoid being taken to the European Court of Justice in the first place. And the best chance of achieving this is to treat the infractions process seriously from the start. As a rule of thumb, the workload for officials in the Member State administrations triples at each successive stage of the infractions process, and time invested at the early stages is well spent. The UK Government policy is to seek to settle infraction cases, though not at the expense of principles such as the respective spheres of competence which fall to Member States and to the Community.

An infraction case may allege a breach of Community law for a matter not under the direct control of the government (for example, a planning decision taken by a local authority or an unauthorised discharge of pollution from a factory), but the case will still be against the UK authorities. It is usually best to be open with the Commission in such circumstances. If the Member State government can be shown to have acted promptly to deal with the problem, the chances of the Commission closing the case are much improved.

---

**Spanish Monkeys**

Infraction cases may often seem only a burden to UK officials. They also, though, protect and extend the rights of individual citizens. Nor is the UK the only recipient. One story doing the rounds in the Commission tells of a Spanish organ-grinder touring the holiday resorts. The Commission officials could plot his progress up the coast by the letters of complaint received from British holiday-makers outraged that he had a Capuchin monkey dancing on top of the organ.

---

*The Origins of Infraction Cases*
The Treaty gives to the European Commission the duty to protect the rule of Community law (Article 155). It is given

specific powers to allow it to investigate possible breaches of Community law on the part of Member States (Article 5) and, where appropriate, to refer these to the ECJ (Article 169). So, while individuals and other Member States can have recourse to the ECJ and to national courts to enforce Community legislation in certain circumstances, prime responsibility, both in theory and practice, falls to the Commission: hence the concept of the Commission as the 'Guardian of the Treaty'.

So the Commission has a duty to protect Community law. It does not, however, have many staff or effective mechanisms to monitor implementation in Member States: in 1996 the legal unit in DG XI (Environment) had only one official working on UK infractions. The technical and scientific resources are equally sparse. The main source of infraction cases is not the Commission itself but the vast number of outside complaints it receives each year.

Any citizen or pressure group can write to the Commission to complain about any act of any Member State government: the Commission considers itself bound to assess and, where necessary, investigate such complaints. Many may well be unjustified, but the Commission is often not well placed to know this: if a UK citizen writes to the Commission alleging that the UK Government has approved an open-cast mine in, say, Hyde Park without a proper assessment of the environmental impact (contrary to Directive 85/337/EC), the Commission official on whose desk the letter lands will be unlikely to know the facts. The obvious course of action for the Commission official is to write a letter of enquiry to the UK Government: a pre-Article 169 letter is born.

Areas such as equal opportunities, employment rights and the environment are naturally of concern to many citizens, and such a simple and cheap possible means of redress is extremely attractive, particularly in the UK, with its tradition of writing to constituency MPs. Action groups such as Friends of the Earth, Liberty and the larger trades unions are also fully conversant with the system and with supporting such letters with scientific evidence and lobbying of Commission officials. Knowledge of the procedure is also spreading: the Council for the Protection of Rural England have produced a handy booklet on the subject.

The European Parliament also plays a role in launching cases. The Commission usually pays attention to the views of MEPs. UK MEPs are particularly likely to pursue cases which concern their constituents. In addition, the EP has a system of petitions (including a Petitions Committee) which can also form the basis of an infraction case.

Member States also have the right to issue a complaint against (or *grass on*) another Member State to the Commission and even, should the Commission not act, to take the Member State to the ECJ. This right, set out in Article 170, is rarely used but not forgotten.

All this said, the ignorance of the Commission itself should not be overstated or relied on. It has various sources of information and on occasions can be better informed than desk-bound civil servants. These sources include:

### Newspapers, radio and television
The UK nationals are delivered in Brussels the same morning. BBC1 and BBC2 are available on cable in Brussels. Radio 4 reception is excellent: one Head of Unit listens to the *Today* programme each morning on his way to work.

### Lobby Groups
The Royal Society for the Protection of Birds, Greenpeace and other major non-governmental organisations either have Brussels offices or European Affairs staff. They often have excellent access to Commission officials.

### Commission Offices
The Commission has offices in London, Cardiff, Edinburgh and Belfast. Their staff are sometimes asked for advice and the local angle on infractions cases.

### Site Visits
Apart from those arranged by the UK Government or protesters, Commission officials (even those who are not British citizens) often know the UK well. One past Environment Commissioner had even spent time in his

youth birdwatching at a site where a proposed development was the subject of a complaint to the Commission under the Wild Birds Directive.

## Breaches of Community Law
There are three broad classes of breaches of Community law: non-notification; incomplete (or faulty) transposition; and incorrect (or faulty) application.

### Non-notification
All national measures necessary to transpose Community legislation must be notified to the Commission (see above). If the Secretariat-General does not receive notification on time, it will open proceedings automatically. Such cases are usually packaged together into a 'jumbo Article 169 letter' and the Cabinet Office co-ordinates the reply.

### Incomplete Transposition
Where transposing legislation has been notified but is judged incomplete or faulty, the responsible Directorate-General may issue proceedings, usually starting with a pre-Article 169 letter. Examples of alleged incomplete transposition often arise as part of a specific case.

### Incorrect Application
This is where a Member State is alleged to have failed to apply Community law properly in one or more specific instances. Many such cases arise from complaints from the public about environmental or planning cases and are usually about *causes célèbres* (Twyford Down, Oxleas Wood) or issues of strong local concern (most cases are about landfill sites, roads projects and waste incinerators).

## Handling of Infraction Cases in the Commission
Infraction cases are based on Article 169 of the Treaty. Around this the Commission has developed a handling system to take cases through the three stages envisaged in that Article: Article 169 letter; Reasoned Opinion; reference to the ECJ. It has also developed a stage before this formal

process: the letter of enquiry known as a pre-Article 169 letter.

### (i) A File is Opened
Proceedings are given a file number when opened by the Commission: A88/0360; P94/4867; C91/0221. The two-figure part is the year the case was opened; four-figure numbers beginning with a '2' are cases generated by the Commission; those with '4' originate with complaints to the Commission; and those starting with an '0' are non-notification cases. Older cases have variations on this pattern. File numbers often have a prefix: 'P' (for 'Plainte') indicates the case is based on a complaint; 'A' that the case has been examined by a special meeting of cabinets; and 'C' that the case is based on an earlier ECJ case (see p. 79 below).

The Commission has been criticised by Member States in the past for failing to close old cases (overworked Commission officials were more concerned with pursuing live actions than tidying up old paperwork and presenting the results to their hierarchy). The Commission's procedures were changed in 1995 to address this concern, and most dormant cases are now closed within a year. Note that writing to the Commission to seek confirmation that a case has been closed can be counterproductive: lawyers, when dusting off the file, may decide to take further action instead.

### (ii) Pre-Article 169 Letters
The formal basis of the infractions system is set out in Article 169 of the Treaty. However, an informal procedure has evolved which often precedes it. This is the pre-Article 169 letter, also known as a Letter of Enquiry. Such letters are issued by the Director-General and set out alleged breaches of Community law, asking for more information or for comments on the allegations. They are intended to avoid unnecessary formal actions, but passing through this stage is not obligatory.

### (iii) Article 169 Letters
These are authorised by the Commission and issued by a Commissioner. They set out the case against a Member State and ask for further information. They are drafted by the legal

unit and cleared by the hierarchy of the DG, the Commission Legal Service and the cabinets. The quality and seriousness of the arguments is usually much higher than for pre-169s.

### (iv) Reasoned Opinions

These are, in effect, statements of the arguments which would be put if the case were to go to the ECJ. They are drawn up by the Commission Legal Service, cleared with the Director-General and authorised by the Commission. Once a Reasoned Opinion has been authorised, the Commission Services are not supposed to discuss ways to resolve the case with the Member State unless this has been specifically allowed by the Commission decision (though they might do so informally). Also, compliance after the period (usually two months) specified in the Reasoned Opinion will not prevent a later judgment against the Member State in the ECJ if the Commission decides to pursue the case. These considerations should not, however, preclude dialogue with the Commission: several awkward UK cases have been resolved satisfactorily even at this eleventh hour.

### (v) References to the European Court of Justice

The Commission Legal Service serves papers on the ECJ in Luxembourg. The lead Whitehall department will assist in preparing the UK's defence, but, by this stratospheric stage, there will be plenty of lawyers around to advise on tactics and procedures. Suffice to say that from 1990 to 1993, the Commission commenced 204 actions against the UK under Article 169, but there were only five UK references to the ECJ. Only Denmark had a better record of compliance with Community law (133 cases and four references).

### Timing

The time which may elapse between each of the stages outlined above can vary enormously. Some cases move rapidly through each stage, but in the majority of cases weeks or months pass between the Commission authorising an infraction letter or Reasoned Opinion and issuing it. The Commission continues to try to speed up the process and now has an unofficial target of eighteen months from the pre-Article 169 letter to a reference to the ECJ. In specific cases, UKRep may be able to throw some light on the course and speed on a particular infraction case.

*Variations*
New information (scientific research, changes to legislation and the like) often emerges during an infraction case. Also, other lawyers are often brought in to look at cases, and their opinions need to be taken into account. Information may be passed over and discussed through a number of formal and informal channels.

Much of this is done by letter: both the Commission and the UK Government can change and extend their arguments between the pre-Article 169, 169 and Reasoned Opinion stages (although arguing contrary to statements made in earlier correspondence is always likely to cause problems: hence the need to get arguments and facts right from the start!). The Commission may also send 'supplementary' pre-Article 169 letters, extending the allegations, even after an Article 169 letter has been sent. Once a Reasoned Opinion has been sent, the Commission would need to issue a revised Opinion, preceded by a revised or supplementary Article 169 letter, if it wanted to raise an argument before the ECJ which was not in the original Reasoned Opinion.

The UK Government can write to the Commission with new information or arguments at any time: any such approach has, however, to consider the tactical advantages of letting sleeping dogs lie. There is also the question of confidentiality. For these reasons, civil servants are not supposed to discuss infraction cases with the Commission or anyone else, by letter or orally, without clearance in advance by UKRep and the Cabinet Office.

*Article 171 Proceedings*
Where a Member State has a judgment against it in the ECJ, and the Commission considers that the Member State has failed to comply with that judgment, it may launch proceedings based on Article 171. The process is the same as for Article 169 proceedings, except that the Commission has to specify 'the amount of the lump sum or penalty payment' to be paid by the Member State. This process was introduced

into the Treaty (at the suggestion of the UK) in 1991, but its first use (against Germany and Italy for failing to implement ECJ judgements on several Directives) was not until January 1997. Judgement on the Commission's application is awaited, and this could have quite an impact: the Commission has, for example, asked for a fine of 264,000 ecu per day for the Groundwater Directive above.

# Chapter 5
# Committees

**Invitation to view Committee Room 12**
*A delightful room, conveniently situated on the fifth floor of the prestigious Justus Lipsius building in downtown Brussels, with views of the attractive office block opposite, and with many of the features of Committee Rooms 1 to 11. Property comprises one chamber complete with uncomfortable leather chairs and a fug of Gauloise smoke, nine en-suite translation booths, and two WCs for real negotiations. Room 12 shares the use of the anteroom, permanently staffed by a surly bloke with a big moustache, and benefits from an extremely effective air-conditioning system which returns the air, still smoky, at about 40°C (in summer) and −40°C (in winter).*
*Price on application − no time-wasters.*

## Committees and Comitology

The Union was not founded merely to pass legislation: it also administers, reviews and updates existing legislation and programmes. Directives and Regulations which need ongoing administration, further subsidiary decision-making or *adaptation to technical progress* (jargon for 'updating') will usually establish a committee of representatives of the

Member States, chaired by the Commission, to carry out these tasks. Anything which seems too detailed for Ministers and MEPs to consider themselves, or which needs to be updated rapidly or without recourse to the cumbersome procedures for amending legislation, may be delegated.

Formally, the parent legislation delegates powers to the Commission from the Council (or from the Council and the European Parliament when legislation is adopted by the co-decision procedure). These powers may be anything from licensing production of certain hazardous chemicals to approving imports of rare orchids or adopting standards for product labels. The committees are set up to assist the Commission.

These committees are significant both for the powers they exercise and for the important role administrators play in their workings (usually without day-to-day help from UKRep). The whole subject is known by the exciting term *comitology*.

Although the Commission and Member States are by far the most significant actors, the European Parliament increasingly plays its part, though the extent to which it does so can be a matter of dispute. Also, the workings of committees are often influenced by lobbyists and other concerned groups.

Comitology is an important subject because:

- technical but controversial issues are sometimes left to committees in order to avoid holding up agreement of the parent measure in Council
- significant management powers, such as the right to set import or production quotas for whole industries, are devolved to committees
- the choice of the type of committee affects the scope for Member States to protect their interests and ensure a sensible regulatory regime, as it modifies the decision-making process within the committee and between the committee and the Council.

The 'comitology' of a proposal must be right from the start: changing the type of committee would mean changing the parent Directive or Regulation. Often, the choice of committee type is decided by Ministers as part of the final settlement at Council.

## Types of Committee

Committees are chaired by the Commission and consist of representatives of the Member States. These committees can have different roles – advisory, management or regulatory – corresponding to different levels of control over the Commission's activities and different procedures for referring disputes between Commission and Member States to the Council. Committee decisions are based on proposals tabled by the Commission.

The workings of these committees are governed by the rules set out in the parent Directive or Regulation which establishes them. In practice, there are five standardised forms: Consultative Committees (Type I), Management Committees (with two variants, Type IIa and Type IIb) and Regulatory Committees (again with two variants, Type IIIa and Type IIIb).

*Type I (Consultative Committees)*
The Commission must seek the advice of the Member States and must take the views of the committee into account. In practice, it would be difficult to force the Commission to change its proposal radically, even if the committee as a whole was hostile. The Commission does not have to forward its proposal to the Council, and while the Council might discuss it at the request of a Member State, it cannot act to overturn it (unless a proposal for a Council Regulation or Directive happens to have been tabled by the Commission on the same subject, and even then the Commission could withdraw that proposal).

However, Member States are not helpless: the Commission will usually be reluctant to offend the Council or individual Member States by cavalier actions. Even an individual Member State may insist on its dissenting view being recorded in the minutes.

## Type IIa and IIb (Management Committees)

The Commission tables proposals which the Member States may vote upon. If there is a qualified majority against the Commission proposal, then the Council may intervene and amend the proposal, again acting by qualified majority. Under the Type IIa variant, the Commission may (or may not) postpone implementation of the proposal for up to a month, while under the Type IIb variant, the Commission *must* delay implementation for a time, usually three months, as specified in the parent legislation.

Under both variants, the Council must act before the expiry of the deadline.

---

**Making Amends**

The usual wording under both Type IIa and Type IIb committees is that the Council 'may take a different decision' on proposals referred to it by the Commission. Similarly, in Type IIIa and IIIb committees the Commission may proceed with its original proposal 'if the Council has not acted'. The Council and Commission disagree on whether this gives scope for the Council (under the Type IIIa procedure) to reject the proposal as a whole: in other words, to amend to nothing.

On occasions, the wording 'if the Council has not acted' has been replaced by 'if the Council has not adopted any measures'. This might look like a variation in translation from, say, the French-language version. However, a moment's thought shows that this new wording means that if the Council rejects the proposal outright, there is no Council 'act' as the Council has not acted in adopting a measure and so the Commission may proceed with its original proposal.

The moral is: **check the exact wording** of a proposal (even when it's standardised!). Once in a Directive, wording such as this cannot be put aside just because of a different interpretation in the inter-institutional agreement on committees. The specific wording in each parent Directive or Regulation, not the 'standard' wording, is what matters.

*Type IIIa and IIIb (Regulatory Committees)*
The IIIa is also known as the *filet* (or safety-net) and the IIIb as the *contre-filet* (or double safety-net). Under both versions, if there is not a qualified majority in support of the Commission proposal, then the Commission must without delay submit a proposal (not necessarily the same proposal) to the Council. The Council may then (within the deadline set by the parent legislation, usually three months):

- **adopt** the Commission proposal by qualified majority; or
- **amend** the proposal by unanimity; or
- **do nothing**, in which case the Commission adopts its own proposal.

The Type IIIb variant has a second 'safety-net': as well as amending by adopting, amending, or doing nothing, the Council may (within the deadline) **reject** the Commission proposal outright. To do this, the Council need only have a simple majority – eight out of fifteen Member States. In this case, the Commission would have to start all over again with a new proposal (but note that the Council still cannot act except on the basis of a Commission proposal).

*The Implications of the Choice of Committees*
As the Commission, broadly speaking, gains most power and flexibility from Type I and Type IIa committees, these are the types usually included in Commission proposals. The UK usually takes the opposite line (that the Commission's actions will be of an even higher level of wisdom and quality if guided by the Member States) and so suggests a Type IIb or Type III committee.

Although the choice of committee affects the balance of power between Council, Commission and Member States, it is not the case that they can be graded neatly from Type I (very good for the Commission) through Types IIa, IIb and IIIa to IIIb (very good for the Member States). The complexity of the voting arrangements and the process for referring disputes to Council means that the appropriate choice of committee can vary. Often, Member States will see their interests as closer to the Commission than to other states on certain issues – say, France on culture or the UK on trade.

All this makes the choice of committee usually quite contentious when the parent legislation is being negotiated. In part this is because it is important, and in part because Ambassadors and Ministers are familiar with the issue, as it is common to so much legislation. Some might even miss the ritual: for example, the Commission will *always* object if the Council wants to impose a Type IIIb, and will insist that the Council acts unanimously to do so.

The key points to remember when seeking to influence the choice of committee are:

- With a Type I committee, you can't refer a proposal to Council, even if the Commission ignore you.
- It is more difficult to refer problems to Council from a Type II committee than a Type III, but once there, it is easier to amend the proposal than under the Type III procedure.
- Once in the Council, it can be very difficult to amend a proposal, and this can lead to problems if questions of drafting have not been resolved. There is a tendency to want to stick with the Commission proposal, warts and all, rather than start negotiating the proposal line by line.
- The Council has very little time to act, which leaves even less time for lobbying and alliance-building.

## Rules of Procedure

These standard forms only give the outline of the committee's working methods: the detailed rules of procedure, such as when proposals can be tabled or whether proxy votes are allowed, are adopted by each committee itself. Helpfully, these rules are rarely made known to the outside world, so following the course of negotiations in these committees can be very difficult. For national representatives serving on these committees this means:

- Be very careful when agreeing rules of procedure when the committee is first established.
- Always keep the rules to hand (ask the Commission for a copy if necessary) to avoid being caught out by some point of detail.

## Membership of Committees

The delegates to Commission committees are usually experts from Member State administrations (central or regional government, research institutes and other public bodies) who have worked in the field for many years and often sat on the expert groups which helped to draft the original Commission proposal. Non-governmental delegates (for example, from campaigning groups or businesses) are not supposed to attend.

Personalities and relationships often play a stronger role even than in the Council working groups, and this can pose a problem for the UK, whose civil servants tend to be rotated between posts more frequently than their continental counterparts. The most effective approach is the rather obvious one of developing personal links with other delegates as quickly as possible without giving up the defence of UK interests where necessary.

Officials also have to deal with apathy on the part of others, not to mention the non-attendance by some delegations (due to lack of staff or cash resources, or even difficulty in travelling: the timing of flights from Athens to Brussels, for example, means that Greek delegates have to take three days away from their offices to spend one day at a meeting in Brussels). It can be difficult to motivate delegations to resist attempts on the part of the Commission or another Member State to railroad through proposals, particularly if the proposal only affects a handful of Member States.

## Practical Considerations

It is vital to keep in mind the attitudes and concerns others bring to the committee table. The Commission official in the chair has a responsibility to pilot the proposal through as smoothly as possible and to defend the ideas agreed across the Commission and often supported by the Commissioners themselves. Remember that there is a great deal of pressure on meeting rooms and interpretation teams: arranging an extra meeting to consider fresh proposals is always likely to be a headache.

Wherever possible, show that the plight of the Commission official is understood and try to pitch your arguments to work with the groove: for example, by pointing out that making amendments to gain your support will make adoption easier.

## Adoption of Committee Decisions

When a proposal has been discussed by committee, the usual practice is for it to be adopted formally by the College of Commissioners. This process is required whether or not the committee has proposed any changes to the original Commission proposal or whether the Commission has ignored any such suggestions or not.

As with any formal Commission act, the usual pattern is for the proposal to go out to inter-service consultation whenever other Directorates-General have a policy interest, and to go through the cabinets. The former stage is often carried out before a proposal is put to the committee.

At both stages, timely lobbying can bring about improvements: at the least, it may result in the proposal being remitted to the committee for further work or otherwise delayed. It is important to keep contacts in the Commission aware of any problems as they evolve within committees: the Commission officials actually attending the committee may not do this. This can be done directly (but be careful about mentioning the lobbying of cabinets) or through other Whitehall Departments (for example, in explaining the problems with a DG VII (Transport) proposal to DG III (Industry) via officials in the DTI). Better still, co-ordinate your efforts with allies on the committee: a joint approach from a number of Member States will have more impact than from one country alone.

## Serious Difficulties

The structure of the standard forms of committee used in legislation can pose difficulties because only a small proportion of the possible situations are foreseen and adequately covered. By way of an example, all five committee types assume that the Commission will bring forward proposals to be considered by the committee: if the Commission does *not* bring forward any proposals, an entire Directive or Regulation can be rendered inoperative.

Similarly, the legalistic use of the Rules of Procedure adopted for a particular committee may prevent Member States from putting forward any proposals at short notice, so that effective negotiations, where improvements or compromises are tabled and discussed, can become impossible.

In such circumstances, the help of others outside the committee may be needed. In the first instance, you should alert UKRep and departmental colleagues to the problem: they can advise on the exact legal position and suggest tactics to avoid the impasse. If the problem is an individual official within the Commission, it may be possible, through unofficial contacts, to persuade others within the Commission (in the same Directorate-General, in other parts of the Commission or in the cabinets) to look into the position. To be effective, such interventions usually need some form of compromise: for example, if the main UK concern were addressed, the UK could in return offer co-operation towards its speedy adoption.

It may be helpful for the appropriate attaché from UKRep to attend part of one of the meetings and, in very serious cases, UKRep can raise the problem in the Council working group.

---

A Member State renowned for efficiency has, by mistake, entered a prestige bid for Community funding in the wrong category. The bid has therefore been rejected by the Commission, but when the decision goes to the management committee to be agreed, the Member State representative, who has attended every committee meeting for eight years, starts the fightback.

**Day One:** the committee is treated to eight hours of discussion, argument and pleading by the delegation. Eventually, the Commission official cracks and agrees to reconsider the bid.

**Day Two:** the other Member States realise this might mean less money for them and so object.

**Day Three:** the Commission agrees to a compromise: they accept the prestige bid, but take the money from the Member State's other bids. The ashen-faced delegates return to their capitals, to the usual jibes from their colleagues about idle jaunts to Brussels.

Remember, finally, that blocking a proposal in committee and sending it to Council has its own risks. There was probably a good reason for the Council to delegate the power in the first place: it may be far too technical or detailed for Ambassadors or Ministers to deal with effectively, and it may also be urgent.

Also, the procedures for handling in the Council are quite rigid: the Council will have three months at most in which to act, and if there is not a convenient Council meeting, a trade proposal might end up at a General Affairs or Fisheries Council instead. The voting arrangements may not be favourable, particularly if the proposal under discussion is flawed. Amending a proposal is difficult under the Type III procedure, and so a duff text might go through by default. This not only affects the choice of committee (a Type II committee might avoid this risk) but also how officials negotiate within it (and other interested groups lobby from outside). Both might benefit from a satisfactory if imperfect deal in committee, rather than forcing a vote and finding a nightmare waiting in Council.

**Entering the Lists**

The Council adopted a Regulation in 1991 which set up a committee and asked it to prepare a list of hazardous wastes. This did not prove easy (which was probably why the Council didn't do it itself). By 1993, the Commission and the Member States had worked up a list, and this was put to the committee formally. The wrangling went on, however, as each Member State had different national practices and the costs of adding a waste category could be enormous.

In the end, the Commission put the proposal to the

vote and lost. The proposal went to the Council, needing agreement by 28 December by the latest. Agreement, though, was not possible. No Member State liked the Commission proposal. Even the Commission didn't like its proposal. But no one could produce a compromise which satisfied all Member States: unanimity was elusive and the wrangling went on. So the Commission withdrew its proposal and tabled another text which could command a qualified majority (there were only twenty votes against), and this was adopted. No one was quite sure if this approach was absolutely legal, but by then most delegations were past caring.

# Chapter 6
# The Community Budget

*The Stereotype family are playing the exciting new board game, BUDGET!:*

TIMMY: *My turn. [Rolls a six.] Oh no, I've landed on rue de la Loi!*

SALLY: *Great. You owe me 420 mecu.*

TIMMY: *No I don't, 'cos I've got a Community Fudge card which lets me claim my rebate under the 1992 Edinburgh Financial Perspective.*

SALLY: *Well, I can counter that with an Inter-Institutional Agreement under Article 203 paragraph 9 of the Treaty. So there!*

TIMMY: *All right, I'll mortgage rue Belliard and claim an extra 1.2 becu under the structural funds.*

SALLY: *Ha, ha! You can't. You haven't got EUROPES cover. It's in the rules.*

TIMMY: *That's not fair! Mummy, Mummy! Sally's cheating.*

SALLY: *But cheating's the whole point of the game!*

MOTHER: *Hush now, children. You'll wake Father.*

FATHER: *Zzzzzzz.*

# Introduction

The Union has a series of programmes intended to achieve its policies. The main classes of expenditure are price support for agricultural produce under the Common Agricultural Policy, the development of disadvantaged areas and groups through the structural and cohesion funds, other internal programmes such as research, and external aid. Though still a huge sum, the proportion of the budget spent on the CAP is declining as more money is channelled into the structural funds.

The Union budget may be less than 2% of the Gross National Product of the Member States, but that's still a vast sum: 82 becu (£59bn) in 1996. Chapter 7 sets out Community spending in more detail, with the latest budget figures shown on p. 111. This chapter explains how the money is raised and allocated through the budget.

# The Budget

The budget is perhaps the most complex and intimidating part of the Union's structure, having its own procedures and jargon. The budget itself weighs in at several kilos, with hundreds of pages of closely printed tables setting the exact amount to be spent on each individual Community programme. Though the budget-setting process can of itself be rather boring, anyone wishing to influence how Community funds are spent, or to bid for individual grants, loans or contracts, needs to be aware of the outline.

## Sources of Community Revenue

The Union raises money from:

- contributions related to national Value Added Taxes (just over 1% of turnover liable to VAT), which raises about £34bn or 49% of the budget (1996 figures)
- levies on imports of agricultural products into the Union and contributions related to customs duties levied at the Union's external border (together raising about 18%)

- contributions from each Member State according to their Gross Domestic Product (about 33%): this source of funding is known as the 'third resource', probably because it was only introduced in 1988

The money that can be raised is capped at a proportion of the Gross National Product of the Union, currently set at 1.2% but set to rise to 1.27% by 1999.

## Setting the Budget

The budget is negotiated by the Treasury and UKRep, but other departments are asked to comment on and, if necessary, supply more detailed briefing on each *budget line* (item of expenditure) for which they have the policy lead. A preliminary draft budget is prepared by the Commission each June and passed to the Council and the European Parliament. After line-by-line negotiation in the working group and Coreper, the July Budget Council then adopts a draft budget by Qualified Majority Voting.

Expenditure is classed either as **compulsory** (mainly agricultural support) or **non-compulsory** (everything else), a classification that determines the scope for the Parliament to change the proposed expenditure. With compulsory expenditure, the EP votes on the draft budget in October and the November Council then adopts or rejects EP amendments as it wishes. However, in the case of non-compulsory expenditure, the position taken by the Council has to go back to the Parliament, which can to a large extent determine the overall level of expenditure and the amount allocated to each budget line.

The Parliament, which with the Council makes up the Community's *budgetary authority*, has extensive powers over the budget. Consequently, this process is in practice much more complicated than appears from the above description because of the need for formal and informal means of consultation. These are governed in part by an *Inter-Institutional Agreement* between Parliament, Council and Commission. In practice, the budget shuttles back and forth between Council and Parliament (with the Commission engaged in the process too) in the search for compromise. This process is sometimes called the *navette* (French for 'shuttle': and yes, the name of Eurotunnel's *Le Shuttle* service irritates the French too).

## Spending on Lending: the European Investment Bank

The Commission does not have the right of itself to borrow or lend, so the Union has the European Investment Bank (EIB), which makes loans within the EU for infrastructure projects (such as roads, railways and other parts of the Trans-European Network programme, and less glamorous projects such as sewage treatment works); other investment (such as Airbus); and to third countries for macro-financial assistance on the basis of individual Council decisions. None of this expenditure appears in the Community's budget, but the budget does bear guarantees for some of these loans, and also may subsidise interest payments in some circumstances, such as for EIB loans for job creation schemes for small and medium enterprises.

The EIB is based in Luxembourg and, with a staff of about 750, lends upwards of 20 billion ecu (or becu) a year (but doesn't lend less than 10 million ecu (or mecu) at a time). The EIB should not be confused with the European Bank for Reconstruction and Development which, though 51% funded by EU states, is not part of the Union. Based in London, the EBRD lends money to help redevelop Eastern Europe (and is famous for its £30m marble cladding).

## Spending on Administration

About 3% of the budget is spent on the staff and other running costs of the Community institutions. Exactly how this is spent is of little direct interest, though pressure to keep down staff numbers has an effect on employment policies: it tends to result in occasional freezes on recruitment; difficulty in filling posts; and the use of staff working under contract as consultants. All this has implications for those wishing to work for the Commission, Parliament or Council (see Chapter 2).

The Commission assesses the financial impact of each proposal it makes in a *fiche d'impact*. This looks first (and often in greatest depth) at the costs to the Commission itself in staff and other resources; only then does it look at the implications for Member States, business and individual citizens. This is because:

- it is not usually in the Commission's interest to show the wider costs of a proposal
- the Commission usually relies on Member States to help compile such estimates and many Member States are either not interested or are incapable of producing reliable estimates
- the costs may be difficult to quantify with any certainty: for example, the cost of fitting silencers to all outboard motors in the EU would depend on how many such motors there were in use, which may simply not be known

BANX

## Spending on Implementation

Finally, it is worth remembering that the Community budget does not include the costs of the implementation of Community action which falls to Member States or to individuals. In other words, if a Directive was adopted by the Council which stated that all doors must be painted green, the Commission programme to monitor and evaluate compliance (costing, say, £1m) would appear in the budget, but the cost of actually painting all doors green (say, £10bn) would not. As the *fiche d'impact* may not detail these costs accurately either, there is a tendency for external costs to be ignored.

This provides an opportunity for negotiators: no one can deny that the financial burden of a proposal on the ordinary citizen or business ought to be assessed and minimised. Anyone is entitled to state their view on this burden, particularly where no realistic assessment of likely costs has been made by the Commission or the Member States. Presentation of such figures is often a key part of a negotiating or lobbying strategy.

Naturally, the cost-vacuum is best filled by accurate and honest assessments based on independent research and sensible assumptions. Ideally, there should be a simple explanation of how the figures have been derived, so that acceptance by others does not depend solely on trust, but also on verification. If these are not available, back-of-an-envelope figures are probably better than nothing. Using deliberate deception or cavalier guesses runs the usual risk of a wider loss of credibility.

# Chapter 7
# Community Programmes

*Cap'n Silver addressed his pirate crew as, cutlasses in hand, they prepared to board the galleon.*

*'There she lies, me hearties. That ship will make our fortunes, ha, ha, ha! Stand by to board her. No quarter asked for or given!'*

*'Hurrah!' they cried. 'Dubloons! ECUs! Pieces of eight!'*

*'Avast, ye swabs. She's not carrying dubloons. 'Tis better than that. Her hold's crammed to the hatches with application forms, d'ye see? TACIS! Interreg II! Objective 1 regional funds! Research and development projects! The wealth of all Europe at our feet!'*

*'But Cap'n,' said Black Spot. 'None of us sea-dogs can as much as write our names.'*

*'Bugger!' said the parrot.*

## Introduction

The Community has a lot of money to spend; and a lot to spend it on. Rather than list all the grants, programmes and schemes available, this chapter describes the main Community **policies** (for agriculture, industry, regional development, training, cohesion and so on) and the **funds** from which money is distributed to achieve them. It also describes the **Community Initiatives** to achieve related objectives, and other significant areas of spending, such as research and development and overseas aid.

This chapter also gives a flavour of the underlying intention behind each: it is easier to obtain money from the Community if you know why the Community wants to give it to you. The key contact points within the UK Government and the Commission are set out; programmes regularly change their conditions and bidding procedures, and these should always be approached early on.

## Community Policies

Chapter 1 explained the main objectives of the Community, as set out in the Treaty. Money is spent by the Community on all of these objectives or policies, but the proportions vary with the relative need for spending and the way the burden is shared by the Community, the Member State governments and individual people respectively. Some measures, such as regional development, are backed up by considerable Community spending, while for others, such as culture, Community funds are comparatively tiny: just a few million ecus. Community legislation often has huge financial implications, but the costs of meeting the obligations fall mainly on individuals and businesses: pollution control measures would be one example of this.

As a rule of thumb, then, the Community spends something on every policy area, but the main expenditure is on agriculture, regional development, and research and development, and it is worth looking at these three in outline. There of dozens of other programmes but this guide can only provide a few examples to show the sorts of areas they cover. Full details, including contact addresses for specialist advice on funds available, criteria, and details of closing dates for applications and so forth, are to be found in a handy booklet, *Sources of European Community Funding*, which is available from the Commission (the address is in Appendix III).

## The Common Agricultural Policy

Now that Europe is self-sufficient in food, and the proportion of the working population engaged in agriculture has fallen below one in twenty, the original aims of the CAP might seem redundant. But in the aftermath of the Second World War, a policy to boost food production to fight famine in Europe and keep farm incomes up to avoid a drift of population to the cities was seen as essential.

The CAP is based on the European Agricultural Guidance and Guarantee Fund, which spends quite a lot of money on guidance (that is, helping farmers to rationalise and improve efficiency on their farms) and absolutely vast piles of money on price guarantee (that is, intervening in the market-place to support farm product prices and thus farmers' incomes).

The CAP has led to manifest absurdities and opportunities for fraud and waste. It is also, and partly as a result, highly political. Recent reform has managed to contain the cost and reduce the waste inherent in huge stores of produce bought by the intervention boards to support the price (the famous grain mountains and wine lakes: now little more than hillocks and puddles). Further reform, though, remains a priority for all interested parties, particularly as the accession of the countries of Eastern Europe (whose farmers produce vast amounts of food and have relatively low incomes) would bust the current system.

## The Structural Funds

The Community uses four funds to promote its policies for regional and social development, which together are known as the Structural Funds:

- The European Regional Development Fund (ERDF)
- The European Social Fund (ESF)
- The European Agricultural Guidance and Guarantee Fund (EAGGF)*

* Only the 'Guidance' part of the EAGGF forms part of the Structural Funds. The 'Guarantee' part is, in effect, the price support element of the Common Agricultural Policy. The EAGGF is also known as FEOGA.

• The Financial Instrument for Fisheries Guidance (FIFG)

The idea is that Structural Fund spending should be co-ordinated to achieve six **objectives:**

(1) the development of poorer regions
(2) assistance to areas in long-term industrial decline
(3) combating long-term and structural unemployment
(4) the integration of young people into employment
(5A) the restructuring of agriculture and fisheries
(5B) the development of rural areas
(6) the development of sparsely populated areas

At the same time, all Community development spending is covered by a number of principles:

• such spending should not replace national or regional spending, but should complement it (known as **additionality**)
• resources should be **targeted** on the groups or areas in most need
• **programmes** should be favoured over individual or one-off projects
• plans, programmes and individual projects should be negotiated and implemented through a **partnership** between the Commission, the Member State central governments, local and regional governments, and the 'social partners' (industry, unions and other representative groups)
• spending should be **consistent** with the economic and regional policies in the Member States
• the project should **accord** with Community law and other objectives, particularly Community environmental and public procurement rules.

**Objective 1:** the development of poorer regions
This covers those regions where economic output (measured by Gross Domestic Product per capita) is less than 75% of the Community average (these are often termed 'less-favoured', 'least-favoured' or 'disadvantaged' areas, rather

than 'poor'). Funding is available from the ERDF, ESF and EAGGF and accounts for about 70% of Structural Fund spending, or a quarter of all Community spending.

Regional development aid falls into three categories: a series of **mainstream programmes** proposed by the Member States and agreed with the Commission (this covers the bulk of projects); **Community Initiatives** (see box) aimed at Community-wide problems and drawing on local ideas and concerns; and a small number of **pilot projects** for inter-regional co-operation. The legal basis for regional development spending is a Council Regulation (the current Regulation covers the years 1995–9). Programmes and forms of assistance for each Member State are set out in Single Programme Documents which are agreed between the Commission, the Member State and the regional authorities.

In the UK, mainstream programmes tend to be large-scale infrastructure works: building or refurbishing roads and railways; tourism facilities such as leisure centres; and the reuse of derelict land and buildings.

---

**Community Initiatives for Regional Development**
These initiatives cover specific policy areas and have jazzy acronyms.

**INTERREG:**  supports inter-regional and cross-border co-operation, and includes the Trans-manche Region, which links Kent, Sussex and the Nord-Pas-de-Calais region of northern France.

**LEADER:**  backs local initiatives in rural development.

**RESIDER:**  assists the economic and social conversion of areas of steel production.

**RETEX:**  does the same for textiles.

**KONVER:**  does the same for the defence industry.

**RECHAR:**  does the same for coal-mining areas.

---

**Objective 2**: areas in long-term industrial decline
This covers regions and parts of regions where the average rates of industrial employment and unemployment are both

above the Community average, and where industrial employment is in decline. Funding comes from the ERDF and ESF.

**Objective 3**: long-term unemployment
Programmes under Objective 3 are aimed at bringing the long-term unemployed, young people, and others excluded from the labour market back into employment, and are funded by the ESF.

**Objective 4**: training for employment
To help workers adapt to a changing industrial climate and new production skills through training, funded by the European Social Fund.

**Objective 5A**: restructuring of agriculture and fisheries
To help farming and fishing communities to adapt to changing circumstances, in particular reform of the Common Agricultural and Fisheries Policies. Funded through the EAGGF and the FIFG.

**Objective 5B**: the development of rural areas
To help rural areas, particularly those with low agricultural or general incomes, to develop and adjust to changed circumstances. Funding is available through the EAGGF, ESF and ERDF.

**Objective 6**: the development of sparsely populated areas
Sparsely populated means a population density of eight persons or less per square kilometre, but can also be translated as 'Sweden and Finland', who otherwise would not qualify for much regional spending but who face particular difficulties in developing their sub-Arctic regions. Only parts of these two Member States qualify under Objective 6.

*Negotiation and Management of the Structural Funds*
Most funding goes on capital projects, although an increasing proportion can now be spent on revenue support (running costs). Funding usually has to be matched from

other sources (that is, the funds cannot provide more than half the necessary money, though this can go up to 75% for some Objective 1 projects).

All individual grants for projects have as their legal basis the Regulation establishing the Structural Funds. The process for allocating funds is as follows:

The Regulation
→ Eligible areas
    → National plans and programmes
        → Single programme documents
            → Partnership committees
                → Projects
                    → Payments

---

The Structural Funds have brought about a great number of physical changes to the Union and its infrastructure, for example:
- 5,500 km of roads in Portugal
- 500,000 telephone lines in Spain
- £17m towards the cost of the Manchester Supertram
- £900,000 towards the cost of the Tate Gallery in St Ives

---

The Commission has three means by which it supervises expenditure:

- Project evaluation (the impact and effectiveness of individual projects)
- Auditing (ensuring financial probity of projects)
- Programme evaluation (the effectiveness of overall programmes)

The Commission also makes use of its regional offices, in Cardiff, Edinburgh and Belfast, to provide information and assessments on individual projects and local circumstances.

*Handling in Whitehall*
The Structural Funds are extremely significant for the UK, comprising about one-third of the government's Single Regeneration Budget. The current arrangements for struc-

tural funding, which suit the UK quite well, are due for complete renegotiation in 1999.

Negotiations on individual projects and on the overall allocation of programmes and designation of regions are handled by the Regeneration Directorate of the Department of the Environment; the Regional Development division in the Department of Trade and Industry; and the Regional Policy attaché at UKRep. Local authorities, often working through the local authority associations, have a specific role in determining the way regional aid is spent, negotiating directly with the Commission alongside the UK Government. Local authorities and other interested parties also seek to influence decisions, and many authorities have representations in Brussels or employ consultants.

Disputes can arise between the Commission and the Member States over the assessment of the various projects and programmes, and over wider or horizontal issues such as: Member States using Community funds in place of money they would have spent nationally (*additionality*); apportioning revenue generated by projects; and setting standard assessment criteria. The main Whitehall departments with an interest are the Department of the Environment (DOE), the Department of Trade and Industry (DTI), the Ministry of Agriculture, Fisheries and Food (MAFF), the Department for Education and Employment (DfEE – responsible for unemployment policy as well as training and education), the Department of Transport (DOT), the Territorials and the Treasury.

**Government Offices**
In England, DOE, DTI, DfEE and DOT have merged their regional offices to form the Government Office network, with the idea of providing better-integrated services. They have imaginative titles such as the Government Office for London, Government Office South-East, Government Office North-West, and have, of course, reduced these to dull acronyms (GOL, GOSE, GO-NW). Each Government Office leads the planning of regional funding and the assessment of individual bids, and those lobbying in support of bids – as well as

those preparing bids and wishing to ensure that they match as closely as possible the priorities of the Government Office – now need to keep in contact with these officials more than their Whitehall-based colleagues.

## The Cohesion Fund

This fund is only available to Spain, Portugal, Greece and Ireland. The aim, as with the Structural Funds, is to promote the cohesion of the Community through investment in the less-developed regions. Compared to the regional funds, the four Member States have more discretion over how the money is spent. Nevertheless, the usual Community rules on competition, public procurement and environment protection apply to Cohesion Fund projects, and the contracts for the works undertaken provide considerable opportunities for construction, engineering, consultancy and other businesses.

## Research and Development

The Community spends nearly 3 billion ecus (over £2bn or nearly 3% of the EU budget) each year on research and technological development under the **Fourth Framework Programme** for R&D. The current programme runs from 1994 to 1998 and is intended to strengthen the Community's base in science and technology, and in particular to bridge the gap between pure science and commercial development of products and processes. This in turn feeds into other Community objectives, notably employment and competitiveness.

Although available for a bewildering range of projects and objectives, research and development spending is concentrated on certain strategic or 'sunrise' industries, such as biotechnology, telecoms, energy and transport. It also has themes, such as the co-ordination of research effort between Member States and internationally, and promoting the mobility of researchers within the Community. As well as trailing R&D programmes in the booklet *Sources of European Community Funding* mentioned on p. 99 above, DG XIII of the Commission also operates an R&D help desk, offering free information on programmes, publications and contact points (tel: (35243) 01 331 61; fax: 01 320 84).

---

**Other Community Programmes**
To give a flavour, here is a random selection:

**ERASMUS:** assists full-time university-level study in another Member State.
**IRIS:** supports vocational training programmes for women for under-represented occupations.
**LEADER II:** promotes innovative and demonstration projects for tourism, the environment, crafts and local services in rural areas.
**LIFE:** (*L'Instrument Financial pour l'Environment*) part-funds environment projects particularly aimed at nature and habitat protection and the development of new technologies.
**LINGUA:** supports the teaching and learning of foreign languages and the exchange of experience and best practice between teachers.
**TIDE:** the Technology Initiative for Disabled and Elderly People.

---

# PHARE and TACIS

PHARE and TACIS are programmes aimed at supporting the move towards more democratic and market-oriented societies in the countries of Eastern Europe and of the former Soviet Union respectively. Together, spending totals £1.6 becu (£1.1bn) bn each year.

PHARE is channelled through the governments of the participating states to help restructure state enterprises, reform public institutions and administrations, develop the energy, transport and telecoms infrastructures, and enhance the environment (and especially nuclear safety). This help takes the form of 'know-how' (consultancy and training), investment support (funding studies, providing guarantees and credit) and direct financing (for essential infrastructure).

TACIS has much the same aims, with more of a slant towards developing market economies through privatisation, reforming agriculture, and developing institutions such as banks and financial markets.

Projects under both programmes are advertised in the *Official Journal*, and there is also a PHARE and TACIS Central Consultancy Register for those seeking such work. The Commission also runs a TACIS Information Office.

## Trans-European Networks (TENs)

A large proportion of the loans made by the Community help to fund the Trans-European Networks co-ordinated by the Community. These form networks of roads, railways, waterways, energy transfer systems, telecommunications and other basic or vital mechanisms designed to promote movement across, and integration of, the regions of the Community. The designation of specific projects (such as an individual road, rail or pipeline development) as components of the various TENs also plays a role in determining spending under the Cohesion and Structural Funds.

TENs projects are in no way exempt from the usual Community controls on competition, public procurement and environment protection (and in particular the Environmental Impact Assessment Directive). The Commission has suggested that the TEN idea could be extended to the environment, setting up networks of sewage treatment plants or waste disposal facilities to be known as *Joint Environmental Projects* (or JEPs).

## Tapping the Funds

Later chapters discuss the arts of influencing the decision-making process in Brussels: lobbying, negotiating, creating alliances, explaining your position, briefing the media and so forth. Bidding for Community funds makes use of some or all of these arts, but there follow a few special considerations.

*The Cost*
Preparing a bid can be expensive, and you ought to consider not only the prize (the money, contract or business you are bidding for) but also the cost of the bid against the chances of winning. Comparing this to putting cash on the 3.30 at Haydock may be taking the analogy too far, but there is an element of gambling in any competitive process. For example, one English county council, with very good European links and even an office in Brussels, has learnt that bidding for some European funds can end up costing more in staff time and other resources than the funds themselves are worth, and now chooses carefully which funds to bid for.

*The Pitch*
Bids tend to be a trade-off between what you want to do with the money and what the body handing out the money wants you to do with it. The presentation of the bid or application is therefore important: you need to know what they are looking for – be it research into astrophysics or the regeneration of abandoned coal mines – and seek to show how you would deliver it. Even simple techniques, such as using in your bid the same terminology as in the Community documentation, can help.

*Partners*
One approach which wins maximum Euro gold stars is joint bids from bodies in different Member States, if only because such co-operation justifies action at the Community level. For many programmes, such as INTERREG (see p. 102), this approach is in effect mandatory.

*Consultants*
Some consultants offer assistance for those bidding for funds or looking to win contracts, and the usual arguments for and against consultants apply (see p. 146). One angle employed by some is to offer contingency terms: that is, no win, no fee. This can look attractive in that it reduces your

initial outlay and your risk, even if the final receipts are eaten into (as you end up paying the costs of others' failed bids as well as your own successful one). However, being offered such a deal may only indicate that you have a very good chance anyway and may not need consultants at all. As with any deal, think carefully before signing up.

## Matched Funding

Sensibly, most Community spending seeks to increase its own effectiveness by requiring funding to be matched from other sources: the private sector, charities, local and regional government or wherever. The rules for other contributions vary from scheme to scheme, but typically funding will be limited to 50% of the total cost of the project (the Commission will check carefully before handing over the cash and may ask for their money back if the rules are bent). The credibility of the sources of matching funding can be critical to a successful bid. Also, starting off the bidding process without having such funding (or a shrewd idea that it will appear) can be another way of ensuring you waste your time and money on an unsuccessful bid.

## Slicing Up the Cake

Finally, it is worth remembering that most Community negotiations are, to a large extent, open to 'win-win' solutions: that is, they can be settled in ways that benefit both sides. However, negotiations over funding are much more likely to be 'win-lose' negotiations: one side can only increase its funds at the expense of someone else (but see box). Under these conditions, negotiating is about getting more than your fair share (or even about grabbing someone else's share).

This means that a different approach is often called for: more than ever, there will be a divergence between the rhetoric of negotiations (which will be based on apparently impartial criteria) and the machinations going on behind the public positions (particularly the feverish calculations of how these criteria translate into good cold cash).

**Paper Cod**

Negotiations over a fixed 'cake' should only be a matter of dividing it up: but such an approach lacks imagination. During the accession negotiations for Austria, Finland, Norway and Sweden, fisheries became a focal point for dispute. There just weren't enough fish to go round, and if someone gained more, someone else would lose (and, more impossibly, would be *seen* to lose). So the answer was to create more fish.

Thus was born the paper cod: an allocation of fish to Member States in case, in the future, more fish were found than expected and allowed for in the fisheries quota. These imaginary cod papered over the divisions in the Fisheries Council, allowing a deal to go through.

The Fisheries Council is the best place to observe the process: each year, the dwindling European fish stocks are split up between the Member States in bloody negotiations (remembering the adage that when it's time to cut up a cake, the knives come out).

## 1997 Budget Expenditure

|   | Sub-section | Amount in million ECUs | Per cent |
|---|---|---|---|
| B1 | Agriculture Guarantee | 41,305 | 46.3 |
| B2 | Structural and Cohesion Funds, transport and fisheries | 31,738.5 | 35.6 |
| B3 | Training, Youth, Culture, Audiovisual, Media, Information | 793 | 0.9 |
| B4 | Energy, Euratom nuclear safeguards and Environment | 185.7 | 0.2 |
| B5 | Consumer protection, Internal Market, Industry and TENs | 886.7 | 1.0 |
| B6 | Research and technological development | 3,500 | 3.9 |
| B7 | External action | 5,899.5 | 6.6 |
| B8 | Common Foreign and Security Policy | 30 | – |
| B0 | Compensation, guarantees, reserves | 515 | 0.6 |
| A | Administrative expenditure | 4,283.6 | 4.8 |
|   | Total: | 89,137 | |

# Chapter 8
# The International Dimension

*Yes! Book now for the holiday of a career! With Commission Tours, you can visit any number of exotic locations: Geneva! Nairobi! Djakarta! New York! Brussels!*

*Even better, we don't charge you a penny. For a once-only surrender of competence, we'll take you to meet all sorts of interesting foreign people and we'll even speak to them on your behalf! Just leave all the paperwork to us.*

*Commission Tours. Don't be taken for a ride by anyone else!*

## Introduction

With a population of over 350 million, the European Union is the world's largest trading block and contains four of its seven largest developed economies. Not surprising, then, that it should have an active foreign policy and play an important role in negotiations in international organisations such as the United Nations, the OECD and the World Trade Organisation.

To be precise, it is the European Community rather than the Union which may enter into legal commitments such as international conventions or treaties, as the wider Union is not an *international legal personality*. The three main Community institutions – Council, Commission and Parliament – each have an interest in developing policy in international affairs, and, in order that the positions it takes are coherent and have a sound legal basis, the Community has developed a mechanism for policy co-ordination based on Article 228, but including understandings which have grown up subsequently.

In essence, the Commission negotiates on behalf of the Union in areas of *exclusive Community competence*, and negotiates alongside the Member States in areas of *shared Community competence*. (The Parliament's role is more restricted, but its powers over the budget give it considerable influence.) It can be difficult to define what falls into the sphere of exclusive competence, and in practice this is one of the more difficult areas in the relationship between the Commission and the Member States.

International agreements entered into by the Union may also apply to some surprising territories (French Guiana, for example) and not to others (such as the Channel Islands). The boundaries of the Union and the status of territories on its legal margins are as complex as the histories of the Member States themselves.

## International Negotiations – The Legal Basis

Every external action of the Community must have a legal basis, just as for internal procedures. Various Articles of the Treaty, such as Article 113 and Article 130s, can be used as the basis for international negotiations and agreements. When the Commission intends to participate in an international negotiation it should first adopt a draft mandate, setting out its objectives, for the Council to consider. So long as the principle is agreed (usually in Coreper), the Council does not need to adopt the mandate formally (either as it stands or modified) because only one single legal act is necessary to give legal force to the whole procedure of negotiation, conclusion and ratification. It makes sense for this legal act to take place at the end of the negotiation: it is at this point that the European Parliament would usually be consulted.

## Negotiating

On the basis of its mandate, the Commission negotiates on behalf of the Community. Some areas (such as international trade relations) are the exclusive competence of the Community, but in other areas (such as environmental protection) competence is shared between the Community and the Member States. It can prove impossible to distinguish these areas as, for example, the very title of the Washington Convention on the International Trade in Endangered Species (CITES) shows. When does limiting trade in a species stop being environmental protection and start being a trade measure? The opportunities for unseemly tussles over the microphone would be endless.

Therefore, in negotiations where the division of competence is not clear, the Commission and Member States usually reach a *modus vivendi* at co-ordination meetings held before and/or during the negotiations themselves. Usually this on-site co-ordination (in French, *concertation sur place*) means that the Commission presents the Community's position and negotiates on its behalf on areas of exclusive Community competence, and the Presidency does the same for areas of shared competence, unless the co-ordination meeting agrees that the Commission should do so. Alternatively, the Presidency may speak on all matters, whether exclusive or mixed competence. Both the Commission and the Member States may speak in support of or add to the Community's position for their respective areas of competence, and in addition, Member States may speak in respect of their dependent territories. However, Member States should not speak for themselves in such a way as to undermine the Community's common position on any issue.

Such arrangements depend to a great extent on the subject matter at issue and the personalities on the Commission and

Member State delegations. For example, a legalistic Commission official might argue for the right to speak on areas of supposed exclusive Community competence, while a weak Presidency (or even one not present: some smaller Member States might not be able to field anyone for meetings in a more remote location such as Nairobi) may not resist such demands.

The Member States usually try to work with each other and with the Commission: the legal position is not well suited to anyone standing on their rights unnecessarily, and the Community will have much more leverage by acting in concert. Nevertheless, the right to speak independently as a Member State remains.

---

**Creeping Community Competence**

Commentators occasionally suggest that some Commission officials may from time to time look for the opportunity to extend the competence of the Community (and so the Commission) on international affairs by means of precedent: in other words, if they once slip something through it becomes established practice. One antidote to such aspirations is to include in the text of any agreement an article which protects the particular status of the Member States and *regional economic integration organisations* (code for the Community). This example comes from the Convention on Biological Diversity (Article 34.3):

*In their instruments of ratification, acceptance or approval, the organisations [i.e., the Community] shall declare the extent of their competence with respect to the matters governed by the Convention or the relevant protocol.*

---

## Ratification

Once agreement has been reached in an international negotiation, it is common for the resulting treaty or similar instrument to come into effect when a certain number of countries have ratified it nationally. In any case, where an instrument places legal obligations on the Community, then Community law must be modified to give it force, by means of a Directive or Regulation proposed by the Commission and adopted by the Council or the Council and the Parliament in the usual way.

## International Fora

The EU has relations with most countries on earth, and with dozens of organisations, from the largest (the United Nations) to the most obscure (the Agreement on Small Cetaceans of the Baltic and North Sea). These include:

*The Organisation for Economic Co-operation and Development (OECD)*
The OECD exchanges information and promotes co-operation between the world's twenty-five or so richest countries. Based in Paris, it has specialist committees which prepare Decisions and Recommendations for adoption by the OECD Council. OECD work ranges from comments on the economic performance of countries to the Basel Convention classification system for hazardous wastes.

*The Council of Europe*
Founded in 1949 and based in Strasbourg, the membership of the Council of Europe includes the Member States of the EU and EFTA, and also the countries of Central and Eastern Europe (CEECs), Andorra, Malta, San Marino and Turkey. The Council works by consensus and has an Assembly and a Committee made up respectively of parliamentarians and Foreign Ministers from the member states. Both can advance the political process through non-binding resolutions or recommendations. The Council of Europe also initiates Conventions which are binding on those countries which ratify them: the European Convention on Human Rights is one example (see Chapter 2).

*The European Free Trade Association (EFTA)*
The origin of EFTA is reflected in its name: its purpose was to promote free trade between its members rather than establish a common market with common external tariffs and full economic integration; and it was constituted as an association rather than the ever-closer union foreseen in the European Economic Community. Six of the original members when it was established in 1960 (Austria, Denmark, Finland, Portugal, Sweden and the UK) have since left to join the EU. Three of the four surviving members (Iceland, Liechtenstein and Norway) remain in EFTA but have joined the European Economic Area (see below), so only Switzerland is now outside the EU/EEA umbrella. See Chapter 1 for more.

*The European Economic Area (EEA)*
The EEA, established in 1994, was devised in part as a halfway house to membership of the Union. It confers many of the rights and obligations of EU membership on the member states (Iceland, Norway and Liechtenstein) but is a step away from full integration.

The basic right conferred through EEA membership is open access to EU markets for goods and services (the *four freedoms* of the Treaty). In return, much EU law, including most single-market, health and safety, and environment legislation, applies in the EEA states. However, the EEA does not in practice have the weight to use the formal structures for consultation on new legislation to shape that legislation effectively. Decisions are seemingly taken in Council and Parliament without much attention being paid to the views of the three EEA states: indeed, these states do not even have formal access to working papers of the Council (though naturally they obtain then from friendly EU Member States).

Thus, legislation which applies in Norway, Iceland and Liechtenstein may be drafted and agreed in Brussels by fifteen other states and a Parliament in which the citizens of these countries are not represented. It seems inevitable that before long this rather bizarre position will change.

*Other International Fora*

The International Labour Organisation (ILO)
Founded in 1919 and based in Geneva, the ILO brings together governments and employers' and workers' representatives to set standards for employment.

The International Atomic Energy Authority (IAEA)
An intergovernmental body linked to the UN which sets non-binding standards for radiological protection, including those for the management of radioactive waste.

The International Maritime Organisation (IMO)
Based in London, the IMO is responsible for maritime standards and safety and the control of maritime pollution.

The United Nations Economic Commission for Europe (UNECE)
This body has fifty-four members, including most West and East European countries, the United States and Canada. It is multinational and works through conventions binding on those members who ratify them, such as the 1979 Convention on Long-Range Transboundary Air Pollution.

The World Health Organisation (WHO)
In addition to its role in fighting disease, the WHO sets international non-binding standards for the protection of human health in areas such as air and marine pollution, and for hazardous chemicals.

## The Margins of the Union – Member States' Relics

Several Member States have special arrangements for their remnants of empire (see Articles 131 to 136 and Annex IV of the Treaty). These are significant in two ways: they can affect policy, and any arrangements for such territories could have implications for the treatment of British possessions such as Gibraltar and the Channel Islands (see p. 128). Most of these special arrangements are set out in the Treaty, but their implications are not obvious to the lay reader, and in specific cases it may be best to take legal advice.

France probably has the most extensive possessions: these

include French Guiana and several other DOM/TOMs (*Départements ou Territoires D'Outremer*) scattered around the globe, from the coast of Canada (St Pierre et Miquelon) to the Pacific (Mururoa Atoll). The Netherlands has Curaçao and other possessions in the Caribbean; even the ghost of Denmark's empire still lingers in the special arrangements for Greenland.

# Chapter 9
# Co-ordination in Whitehall

*[Captain Slogg is on the bridge of the ESS Enterprise, talking to Science Officer Spock: half-man, half-Explanatory Memorandum.]*

SPOCK:      *It's another Directive from Starfleet, Captain.*

CAPTAIN:   *I'm beaming down to the planet's surface. I can negotiate with the Commission. We have to try to make contact with all alien life forms.*

SPOCK:      *You can't do that, Captain. We have to speak to the Scots first.*

SCOTTY:    *Aye, Cap'n. My Office can'ne allow it!*

CAPTAIN:   *But Scotty, I need clearance.*

SCOTTY:    *Aye, but it'll taek three years tae implement yon Directive.*

CAPTAIN:   *You've got six hours.*

SCOTTY:    *I'll do mae best.*

## Introduction

The final piece of the European jigsaw is the way the Union and its institutions work with the UK administration. This link is crucial: legislation is negotiated by government departments, and once in place the Commission relies

heavily on it to administer Community funds and programmes. This chapter therefore sets out the role of UK
Government departments (conveniently if misleadingly
called Whitehall), and in particular how different departments co-ordinate their work to create the 'government
position'.

In negotiations, no one department can play a lone hand.
There is no shortage of players with a stake: other departments; the Scottish, Welsh and Northern Ireland Offices
(known collectively as the Territorial Departments); UKRep;
the Cabinet Office; No. 10; and various parts of the FCO.
Even within a department, much effort goes into co-ordination between policy officials, European co-ordinators, legal
advisers and other colleagues. These consultees may sometimes resemble those helpful people who crowd round any
game of chess, leaning over to suggest which piece to move
or explain why your plan of attack is doomed. They are,
however, a fact of life.

## The Whitehall Web

There are three Whitehall central co-ordinating bodies for
European affairs: the Cabinet Office European Secretariat;
the EU departments of the FCO; and the UK Permanent
Representation in Brussels. Together, they monitor and
evaluate policies both individually and against the UK's
overall interests and objectives. But all have limited resources and wide remits. The system depends on the vast bulk of
co-ordination being carried out by and between individual
officials in Whitehall departments. The initial and main
responsibility lies there.

Most departments have a central co-ordinating division
for European matters to provide a strategic focus as well as
advice, more formal guidance and other forms of support.
They usually have a specific and stronger co-ordinating role
in dealing with departmental business at Coreper and
Council, including commissioning, preparing or at least co-
ordinating the briefing for Ministers.

Co-ordinating divisions often have policy responsibility
for strategic and cross-cutting European issues such as

subsidiarity, implementation and infractions; represent the department on Whitehall committees; and manage relations with other Member States and the EU institutions, including bilateral meetings, ministerial correspondence and press and publicity.

## The Cabinet Office

The European Secretariat is the co-ordinating body across Whitehall for all EU business. The Secretariat is small (one official might shadow four or five departments) which makes for good horizontal vision. Naturally, the Secretariat cannot follow all dossiers in detail, and any questions of policy or co-ordination have to be flagged up clearly.

Disagreements between departments on European policy are settled by an exchange of letters between Ministers or by the relevant ministerial committee (usually EDE or OPD(E)). These committees proceed either by exchanges of correspondence summed up in a letter by the Minister chairing the committee or, in difficult or urgent cases, by a meeting of Ministers, by decision by the chair of the committee or even by the Prime Minister. Note that OPD(E) is chaired by the Foreign Secretary and that the EU departments of the Foreign Office (who advise him or her) therefore play an important role in its work.

The system is designed to prevent such disagreement or for it to be resolved by civil servants. At the official level, the Cabinet Office has these formal co-ordinating mechanisms:

**European Questions (Officials) Committee (EQ(O))**
Meetings of EQ(O) are intended to resolve conflicts between departments or to allow for collective policy formulation, usually on a specific issue or proposal. They are chaired by the Cabinet Office and are open to all departments. Usually a department is invited to submit a paper for discussion. Minutes of the meeting are circulated (usually within twenty-four hours), including any conclusions and action points.

**EQ(O)L**
Similar to EQ(O), but held to consider legal questions, again usually on the basis of a paper. Participants are usually lawyers, but, as the division between legal and policy questions is rarely clear-cut, administrators sometimes attend. Cabinet Office Legal Advisers (COLA), the Lord Chancellor's department and other 'legal' departments have a strong interest.

**EQ(S)**
Again, similar to EQ(O), but comprising senior officials as a final chance to resolve issues before they are put to Ministers.

**Ad Hoc Meetings**
These are similar to EQ(O)/EQ(O)L but are often called at short notice and do not have a formal EQ(O) paper to discuss: previous papers and correspondence are used instead.

**'Wall/Bender' Meetings**
Co-ordination meetings held in London each Friday between the head of the European Secretariat (currently Brian Bender) and the UK Permanent Representative (currently Sir Stephen Wall). (The name changes with the official.) Senior officials from other departments attending as appropriate. These meetings consider serious and immediate problems and are able to determine courses of action at a high level. The Secretariat produces a note, usually on the same day. Items can be added by Cabinet Office and UKRep.

The Cabinet Office also operates, less formally, as honest broker when departments have policy differences which are proving difficult to resolve. Together with the FCO and UKRep, they have the task of ensuring that the UK position in Community negotiations is in line with UK Government objectives and takes into account the concerns of each department. The Secretariat also has responsibility for horizontal European issues. Amongst these are certain very active dossiers which are of key importance (and are areas into which officials stray at their peril). These inevitably vary over time but usually include:

Subsidiarity
Community competence
Implementation and enforcement
Deregulation
The Inter-Governmental Conference (IGC)

The Secretariat also services the various ministerial committees which deal with European business, including OPD(E), the main committee for European business.
The Cabinet Office provides other departments with

definitive advice on all aspects of Community procedure and policy through a series of guidance notes circulated to departments. This is supplemented by written and oral guidance on any questions arising, particularly on new, sensitive or fast-moving areas. The Secretariat members are, however, extremely busy people, and departments only contact them after consulting the written guidance and departmental European co-ordinators.

The Secretariat are copied relevant papers so that they can keep abreast of developments and spot links to other dossiers and developments, and particularly emerging differences between departments. In addition, the following documents are always cleared with them in draft:

- Correspondence with European Commissioners that has significant implications for other departments
- Major policy documents with a European dimension
- Material with significant implications for sensitive horizontal issues

## The FCO EU Departments (EUD(I) and EUD(E))

The Foreign and Commonwealth Office has overall responsibility for UK policy towards the Union. EUD(I), the European Union Department (Internal), leads on internal Community matters, and its main tasks are:

- Ensuring consistency in negotiating stances and policies
- Providing advice and briefing for Foreign Office Ministers and the Prime Minister
- Policy formulation on EU matters
- Briefing FCO overseas posts (including UKRep) and issuing instructions on lobbying or negotiations

The EU Department (External) (EUD(E)) carries out the same functions for external Community matters, including foreign trade, external economic relations and aid. As a rule of thumb, EUD(I) or EUD(E) is copied in, consulted or alerted in the same circumstances as the Cabinet Office.

As well as the UK Representation to the EU (see below), the various UK embassies and other diplomatic missions overseas can play an important role in EU negotiations. These posts have good contacts in the administrations of their host countries and, particularly in the larger embassies, will have specialist staff covering areas such as trade, science and technology, or agriculture. They are therefore well placed to report back on the intentions of other Member States and to pass on messages from the UK.

Significant papers, and particularly defensive briefing in advance of major and controversial announcements with a European dimension (and 'dimension' would be interpreted quite widely: for example, an announcement about the nuclear facilities at Sellafield is likely to be of great interest to European partners), would be copied to the relevant attachés in the British embassies in the capitals of other Member States (jargon: all EU posts), and to UKRep. Papers might also be copied to the UK missions to Geneva and New York (for international negotiations in the UN), and to the embassies to the countries of the European Economic Area and Central and Eastern Europe.

## The UK Permanent Representation to the European Union (UKRep)

UKRep is the UK's embassy to the European Union. It has about forty desk officers, each dealing with the work of one or more Councils, and is divided into Sections:

**Institutions:** horizontal issues and relations with the EP
**Agriculture:** including fisheries
**Legal:** legal advice, implementation, infractions (except environment infractions)
**Industry:** Industry, Internal Market, Consumers, and Transport Councils
**ECOFIN:** ECOnomic and FINance Council, customs and the budget process
**External Relations:** foreign and security policy; trade policy
**SER:** Social Affairs and Environment Councils and regional policy, health, education, culture, etc.

Each Section is headed by a Counsellor, with day-to-day work for each Council carried out by one or more desk officers (also known as First and Second Secretaries).

The role of UKRep desk officers is to:

- Lead negotiations in the working groups
- Brief and advise Ministers and Ambassadors, particularly at Council and Coreper
- Report on Council, Coreper and other meetings
- Give strategic and tactical advice to Whitehall
- Provide guidance on EU procedures and policy developments
- Report back policy and other developments in the Commission
- Influence staffing and appointments in the institutions
- Lobby and influence the other Community institutions and Member States
- Handle formal matters such as notification of legislation and infractions
- Pass Council working documents and other papers back to Whitehall
- Arrange visits and meetings with senior Commission officials/MEPs

UKRep desk officers have little time to spare for general enquiries from home departments or to be briefed or lobbied by outside organisations, so requests for help have to be brief and to the point. As with the Cabinet Office, try other options first whenever possible.

While responsibility for policy always remains with the lead official, UKRep attachés are responsible for the negotiations. In practice, the relationship between the two is usually a partnership: UKRep providing tactical advice, knowledge of the whole picture on the work of a specific Council and on European affairs, and presentational and advocacy skills. The UKRep attachés also have a lot of experience on tactics within negotiations, with a feel for what will work and what will not.

This said, the attachés are spread quite thinly, and on most dossiers officials from the lead department will spend a lot of time lobbying the Commission or Parliament or contributing to working groups (though some informal and sensitive contacts with the European institutions are best left to attachés).

## The Territorials

The British Royal Family traces its descent from the House of Cerdic, rulers of Wessex from the seventh century. The Kingdom of Wessex has gone a long way since then, mainly by conquest: each century has seen bits added and, increasingly, broken off. Most parts were incorporated more or less into the English and, later, the British state. Others retain an odd status.

This history has shaped the present British constitution, and one consequence is that legislation negotiated by a department responsible, in the main, for England has to be applied in Scotland, Wales and Northern Ireland. That is why the departments with direct responsibility for these areas – the Scottish, Welsh and Northern Ireland Offices – must be kept fully informed about negotiations, so that they can contribute to policy formulation fully and sound the alarm if necessary. Collectively, these departments are known as the *Territorials*.

There are also other parts of the British state which need to be considered: Gibraltar; the Isle of Man; the Channel Islands; and the UK Dependent Territories and Colonies. Keeping their interests in mind in negotiations is less obvious but, potentially, just as important.

## Gibraltar, the Isle of Man and the Channel Islands

Gibraltar is, for certain purposes, part of the European Union. The extent of those purposes has been disputed (officials take great care in discussing this issue with the Commission), so in practice you should assume that any proposal might have some impact. The sponsoring department is the Foreign and Commonwealth Office (Southern Europe Department).

The two main considerations with Gibraltar, and with

Wales, Scotland and Northern Ireland for that matter, are
the **burden** on administrations and on businesses and
individuals which legislation might pose; and the **timetable**
for transposition and implementation. Often the administrations in each area wait for the lead or sponsoring department to produce draft transposing legislation before starting
work on theirs, which makes a short (12–24-month) transposition deadline very difficult to meet.

The Isle of Man and the Channel Islands, by contrast, are
not part of the European Union. They do have a customs
union with the rest of the UK and so with the Union, but no
Community legislation applies there: nor are they eligible
for structural or other funding. The sponsoring department
is the Home Office. That these islands are not part of the
Community is not often appreciated in the other Member
States or the Commission, nor, for that matter, in the UK.

The rest of the remnants of the British Empire is not part
of the Community. Very occasionally some legislation,
particularly that with a large international content, will
affect Bermuda or the South Sandwich Islands or wherever.
The FCO is the lead department.


## Co-ordination Within Whitehall

Co-ordination is supposed to be automatic: you simply copy
the right papers to the right people. (In the real world, of
course, it's more difficult.) The right papers include:

Submissions to Ministers
Statements of policy
Council documents and compromise texts
Reporting telegrams
Notes of the working group discussions

Most officials copy widely: recipients can always ask not to
receive papers. The basic rules are:

- **Always** send papers to the departmental co-ordinators,
  lawyers, UKRep and the other core members of the
  negotiating team.

- **Discuss** copy lists with colleagues to avoid missing out other departments.
- **Consider** whether HM Treasury, FCO and the Cabinet Office should be copied in (for example, if financial, taxation or horizontal issues are at stake).
- **Remember** those departments which are often neglected, such as the Territorials.

For civil servants, the main point in keeping others informed, from a selfish or departmental point of view, is to try to avoid new objectives being brought into the UK position towards the end of a negotiation. In such a situation, negotiating capital has to be shifted away from the main policy to help win these other points. When such issues arise at the last moment, it makes it more difficult to assess relative priorities and other options so effectively. It may well prove impossible to secure these new objectives, or other aims will be sacrificed: all very unsatisfactory.

> The key is to keep others informed: the same techniques used in consulting the public and interested parties outside government (see p. 153) can be used just as effectively inside Whitehall.

For this reason, copying papers is not necessarily enough. The **implications** of proposals often have to be made clear. Draft Directives and Regulations are often hideously complicated when they emerge from the Commission, while the process of negotiation usually tortures them further. They also make use of technical terms and jargon. For outsiders, even in other departments, it can be very difficult to spot the implications for a proposal in their specific fields. It can be just as difficult for those immersed in the detail, let alone while being buffeted by all the strains and pressures of a negotiation. Once again, discussion of this point as part of the team-working meetings may help.

**A Blockage on the Line**
It is 1993. Agreement on the controversial Landfill

Directive is expected at the Environment Council in a few weeks' time. Then an eagle-eyed expert spots a hidden time-bomb: the proposal, as worded, could require British Rail to apply for a landfill licence to cover the deposits on the tracks from every toilet on every train in Britain. Disaster! Papers have been copied to the Department of Transport but the complexity of waste legislation means they missed the implication. A bit of negotiation in the working group and the offending wording is made safe: a nasty departmental clash days before Council is averted.

The answer is to flag up and explain these implications as far as possible: it may take considerable time and effort to have to do the thinking for other departments but it is likely to pay dividends both in achieving your policy aims and in avoiding major hassles in the end-game of the negotiations. It may be unjust, but it seems to be a fact of life that copying papers religiously to other departments, even gaining their adherence to a negotiating line, is no defence to the same department turning round at the last minute and making a royal fuss.

Few Member States have such an elaborate system for consultation, both within and without government, as does the UK. This brings with it several important benefits (though, naturally, it has its down-side). Chief amongst them is that, once the policy has been agreed, one department can demand full co-operation from all the others in seeing it through. Ministers can go to Council with a line which they know can be delivered by the rest of the machinery of government. Ministers in some other Member States may look for legislation which can then be used to persuade their reluctant colleagues at home to follow a policy 'because there is a qualified majority'.

Finally, remember that good government co-ordination carries with it the risk of placing the UK out in front of other Member States, who are able to hide behind or *slipstream* the UK. This danger can be reduced by working with other departments, so that they wind up their opposite numbers in the other Member States and point them in the direction of the problem. For more on this, see Chapter 13.

On this tactical note, we can move from looking at the mechanics of the Brussels machine to how to make it work in practice.

# PART II
# NEGOTIATING AND LOBBYING

# Chapter 10
# Influencing the Decision-making Process

*Winnie the Pooh was sitting at home one day, counting his pots of honey, when there was a knock on the door. It was Rabbit. 'Hello, Pooh,' said Rabbit. 'I've come to take your honey away.' 'Oh,' said Pooh. 'Whatever for?' 'Because I had a Busy Day yesterday. Important Things happened. I decided honey is Bad for you. And I've written out this Directive, and everyone agreed, and so there we are.'*

*'I didn't agree,' said Pooh, in a small voice.*

*'Too late for that now,' said Rabbit. 'Owl wrote it out in the OJ. And Christopher Robin's ratified it by the necessary majority.'*

*'I suppose,' said Pooh, 'this just shows what happens to Bears of Very Little Brain!'*

## Introduction

Readers who have battled through the complex and, on occasions, rather dull descriptions of the European Union in the preceding chapters can breathe more easily. From now on, this guide concentrates on **action**: preparation, devising your strategy, negotiating, lobbying, briefing. Tracking down sources of information, booking hotels, identifying possible allies. How to speak effectively in meetings or prepare a position paper for the European Parliament.

---

It should also be clear by now – if it wasn't already – why you need to influence the decision-making process in Brussels. Take just four areas:

**Legislation**
Brussels adopts dozens of pieces of primary legislation each year, ranging from setting visa requirements to protecting migrating birds from hunters.

**Justice**
There are hundreds of cases each year in the European Court of Justice which clarify the rights and duties of each European citizen and business on everything from employment law to the collection of VAT.

**Administration**
Thousands of individual decisions are made on product safety standards, prices for agricultural products, what makes an eco-friendly toilet roll, bans on hazardous chemicals, or registration of trademarks and patents.

**Expenditure**
Millions of pounds are spent each week on projects: scientific research, roads and railways, cleaning up contaminated land, development aid in Africa and Latin America, tackling drug-addiction, planting trees in cities, restoring historic buildings, and so on.

---

## Preparation

As with any campaign, proper planning and preparation is crucial. The British tradition of muddling though is consigned to history: instead, the watchword is **realism**. The greatest danger in trying to influence others is failing to be clear and realistic about what you want and the chances of getting it.

This starts with your **objectives**: what outcome do you want? Are you at all likely to get it? And what fall-backs, compromises and interim solutions would meet your main concerns? Don't be absolutist: in European negotiations, complete victories are as rare as utter defeats. However well you do, you will never win everything, and however much you are outmanoeuvred, you can always gain some worthwhile consolation prizes.

Once you have a clear idea of your objectives and their relative priorities, you can start to plan how to achieve them. First, you need to review your physical **resources** and, in particular, your negotiating team: are your and their skills, knowledge and experience up to the task, and if not, what is to be done? Also, what sources of information might you make use of to support your case and help put that case across?

At the same time, you need to look for **allies** – co-ordinating with those who share your concerns or objectives, and working on those who might be won over to your position. You should also assess potential objectors, rivals and other problems ahead.

All this forms the foundations for your **negotiating strategy**. Working on the basis of the timetable of the decision you wish to influence, be it a piece of legislation or the award of a grant or contract, you can start to plan:

- when formal negotiations will take place
- how to gather information on the position of others
- when lobbying of key players would be most effective
- the preparation and circulation of position papers or compromise texts

This is the subject of the next two chapters: practical preparation, including guidance on additional sources of information and assistance; and preparing your negotiating strategy.

## Influencing

Your preparations in hand, you can begin to try to influence the process. For this, you have three broad means to hand: negotiating, lobbying and briefing, each dealt with in subsequent chapters (see box).

---

### Negotiation

Meaning discussions in formal circumstances, such as meetings with the Commission, in the Council and its working groups, and debate in the Parliament. Note that negotiations in Brussels usually have more than two sides: commonly there will be fifteen Member States, the Commission and the Parliament, each with positions of their own.

### Lobbying

This is the process of informal influence over the other players in the negotiation and on outsiders with their own powers of influence: explaining the context of the proposal and how it will affect you; creating a good impression for you and your position; on occasions, knocking the opposition by commenting on their public pronouncements or their real position. Distinguishing lobbying from negotiation is a little artificial, but everyone in Brussels knows what the difference is and does the same.

### Briefing

Both lobbying and negotiating make use of briefing, both written and spoken. Briefing is, in effect, passing on information *as you see it*. The way you present your case can be crucial both to the outside world (a clear summary of your position on paper can be passed on and used by journalists, opinion-formers, allies and the like) and to your own side (you don't want to be sitting on the plane back home thinking, *I wish I'd remembered to mention how much it will cost*).

---

## Logistics

The final chunk of knowledge is the terrain of the campaign: Brussels (and, to a lesser extent, Luxembourg and Strasbourg too). In Chapter 16 you will find the essentials for travelling: how to get there, what it's like, where to stay, eat and buy souvenirs, local information, and what to do if something goes wrong.

## Into Action

Of course, each of us has different needs, and for an illustration of this, we can return to our four passengers, stuck on the Eurostar for the last 100-odd pages.

Ron Noakes has just finished leafing through the Tea-pot Directive, which is written in a style very different from the Westminster legislation he is used to. He also suspects that everything else on the continent will be similarly unfamiliar and is now, therefore, absorbed in his copy of this guide, reading how negotiations on the Council actually work.

The UK ceramics industry likes the Commission proposal, because British-made tea-pots will then be able to be sold anywhere in Europe without needing further safety tests in each Member State. However, the industry doesn't like the idea of Commission approval of new tea-pot designs (harmonisation of standards): they want approval in one Member State, such as the UK, to be valid elsewhere (mutual recognition of standards). This is the main objective agreed with his Minister and senior management.

Chapter 2, though, has made clear that the proposal will be decided by Qualified Majority Voting, and, being a single-market provision (based on Article 100a of the Treaty), it is subject to co-decision with the Parliament. He'll need to brief the Parliament on the UK Government position, and so Chapter 15 is next on his reading list.

Giles Weathervane is tapping away on his laptop computer, drafting a programme of visits for the executives of his client company to make next week; but he's also worried that competitors may already be moving in on the Polish factory. He needs more information on the Commission's thinking and has just finished planning his strategy, after reading Chapter 12. Now he's rereading Chapter 14, on lobbying, and planning what to ask a key contact in DG 1A over a working breakfast (times are changing).

Kate Queue has finished preparing some new journalistic Euro-clichés ('faceless Eurocrats' is out, 'Commissars of the New European Order' is in). Now she is buried deep in Annex III, working out which officials in DG XVI would deal with Gothstanton's REBAGNE application. So far, she has been amazed by how open Commission officials are, compared to their Whitehall counterparts (who usually give her a reception colder than the Arctic winds which habitually sweep Gothstanton's golden beaches). She also wants to cover a Council meeting, and as well as reading Chapters 13 and 17, she is looking through the chapter on logistics to find out which hotels the Ministers stay in. Could be a chance for an exclusive . . .

Beside her, Jane Maple MEP sits knitting, while pondering on her cream tea exemption strategy.

*Mmmm. The first thing is to talk to the Commission Legal Service – I'll speak to Gazzo in the Macmillan cabinet – then I can lean on the DG. He owes me a favour over sheep-meat pricing. Then we'll block it at Inter-Service Consultation, unless the Danes join with DG IV and it goes to Council.*

She needs little help, but she still makes a mental note to look over Chapter 14 to remind herself how the Council itself works. Then she relaxes back into her seat.

*Perhaps I'll talk to that nice young man Mr Bashem at UKRep. And if all else fails, I'll ask Mrs Miggins to chain herself to the Commissioner's Mercedes . . .*

Armed with the knowledge these chapters provide, and bolstered by the cautionary tales and top tips from actual negotiations, you'll be ready to open your own campaign. Chapter 17, therefore, brings you the inside story of one Council meeting, to provide a glimpse of what the process is really like, and to reveal what befalls our four intrepid negotiators when they reach Brussels.

# Chapter 11
# Practical Preparation

*BARRISTER: Mr Perkins. The court has heard that you were caught attempting to board a flight to Brussels, and that you were found to be in possession of certain equipment; namely, a copy of the Treaty of Rome, a list of known Commission officials, a packet of Polo mints, several biros, and a card which reads 'Her Majesty's Government could never agree to this proposal.' I put it to you that the only construction to be put on these facts is that you were intending, with malice aforethought, to negotiate. Do you plead guilty or not guilty?*
*PERKINS: Guilty, God help me! [Gasps, uproar in court, reporters run for the doors, spectators swoon, the usher calls for order, etc, etc.]*

## Introduction

At the very start of a negotiation, be it to adopt a new Directive or to try to win a grant to restore your village pond, the temptation is to get stuck in straight away: to start meeting Commission officials, circulating position papers, wining and dining MEPs. But while such activities are all very sensible and valuable, they are also expensive. Expensive not only in terms of cash (though that too, in any decent Brussels restaurant), but in terms of the time and energy required. It may even harm your position: a meeting with a key player before your case is fully developed could waste a valuable opening.

So all in all, and time allowing, it is crucial to set **objectives** for the negotiation; and to prepare a **strategy** to achieve them. Only then should tickets to Brussels be booked.

At the same time, you need to look at the **practical** side of your campaign, as this too will determine how realistic your aims are. So, while pondering on the grand sweep of destiny that is your objectives, and refining the Napoleonic battle-plan of your strategy, you should give thought to the mundane preparation on which victory is based.


## Planning

To plan effectively, you will need to impose some sort of pattern on the negotiation. The classic is a **timetable**: assessing when each stage of a negotiation is likely to take place, following the process laid out in the Treaty (for the adoption of Regulations and Directives) or elsewhere (as, for example, with applications for grant funding). Once this timescale is in place, other parts of your strategy, such as consulting on your negotiating position or meetings with the Commission or with potential allies, can be pencilled in. Budgets and plans for staffing can follow, and so you have a plan (perhaps even a colourful chart suitable for display behind your desk to impress senior management).

However, more planning than that is needed: timetables in the EU are not always stuck to, and you should give thought to the chances of slippage (and the remote chance of something happening *faster* than planned).

Also, negotiating in the Community cannot be planned in the same exact way as building a car. With a car, you can say, 'It's got four wheels, that's probably enough, let's start the next one.' In negotiations, there is always one more MEP to be lobbied, another interest group to be stirred up, further evidence to be circulated. The opportunities are near to being endless, while resources are, inevitably, limited. This means hard choices have to be made about what can and cannot be done and where resources will bring the best returns.

BANX

Timetables can also give a false impression of steady progress. Community business is much less constant, with proposals stagnating for months or years before accelerating to a breathless finish. This is seen most clearly with grants and loans made under an annual bidding system: there, the pace of the process has peaks and pauses marked out which you must match. Similarly, legislation usually has a rhythm, based upon the pattern of work in the Commission, Council and Parliament.

## The Rhythm of the Negotiation

A typical Council might meet four times a year, which gives four peaks of activity. These peaks are not equal, though: most Council Presidencies use the first of the two Councils held in their six-month term to prepare the ground on the more controversial proposals for agreement at the second (so that they can maximise the chances of reaching an agreement).

Work in the Council is prepared by officials in the working groups and Coreper, and so their work pattern resembles that of the Council, but building more gradually during the preceding weeks. The pattern is important: points of detail are less likely to be considered as the wave rises and the dossier is considered by more exalted officials and, finally, by Ministers. Similarly, interventions can be made too early or, much more commonly, too late. Council meetings last only one or two days and often have a hefty agenda: there is not time for lesser points to be taken, however significant they may be to a particular group or sector, or even a particular Member State.

The same pressure wave affects the Commission officials working on a dossier, and all are affected too by the weekly rhythm of negotiations: the same official who is too busy to discuss a proposal on Tuesday, before a working group meeting on Wednesday, may be relaxed and expansive on the Thursday. Those inside a negotiation, and those seeking to influence it from the outside, have to tune into these patterns.

## Resources and the Negotiating Team

No negotiating or lobbying effort is the work of an individual on a solo mission. Even James Bond (not known for negotiating when an exploding cigarette case would do the job instead) was backed up by 'M', 'Q' and Moneypenny. Any number of lawyers, experts, scientists, administrators and even media and PR people may assist in specific areas, and usually there is a hard core who work on the negotiation as a whole. The constitution of the team depends on the individual circumstances and the personnel to hand, though the box below shows the approach now becoming common in Whitehall.

**In essence, a negotiating team needs to combine the skills of those who know the subject with those who know the system**.

The first is covered by the experts – those who actually know what it's all about, be they engineers, economists, doctors, lawyers, administrators or jam-makers. The second can be covered by the same people, if they know their way around the Brussels machine, or by specialists.

In the UK Government, as Chapter 9 sets out, the UK Representation, the Cabinet Office, the Foreign and Commonwealth Office (FCO) and the European co-ordination units (in those departments that have them) provide specialist support and advice. Others should consider the need for the same expertise: organisations from BP to the RSPB have European experts on the payroll, while others buy in such skills from the outside in the shape of consultants and lobbyists.

Particularly during the negotiation of legislation, lawyers are crucial in establishing the implications of proposals and later amendments. Apart from a knowledge of the subject under negotiation itself, the first need is to include in the team a source of sound advice and expertise on European law. Progress will be nigh-impossible without knowing the implications of the proposals and any later amendments.

---

**Team Working**

Modelled on the Bill teams which work on legislation in Westminster, a typical Whitehall negotiating team for a European Directive or Regulation would consist of:

- the lead official
- his or her immediate colleagues working on the same policy
- administrative support
- a departmental lawyer
- the departmental European co-ordinator

- the responsible UKRep attaché

Representatives from other departments, such as the
FCO or Scottish Office, might also be included. Others
would also be copied in on papers and consulted on
individual points, but the team – meeting as appropriate – would be the motor of the negotiation.

Regular team meetings allow for rapid spreading of information; for consultation and brain-storming; and for a joint
assessment of progress made and tasks remaining (for
example, by reviewing the checklists set out in Appendix
I).

A final thought about team working. The array of specialists – lawyers, negotiators or scientists – should not obscure
the essential role of the expert: that is, the person who
actually knows about the subject under discussion. So much
of negotiation and lobbying is about convincing people, and
for this you need to be able to call on first-hand experience.
You also need to know what matters and what does not, in
terms of the practical application of a measure being
considered. Again, those who would have to live and work
with the legislation are well placed to comment on how it
should be shaped.

## Training

Part of the process of establishing the negotiating team, and
the wider circle who might be called on to assist on specific
parts of the negotiation, is to assess the skills the team will
need, and whether further training is necessary. This
process (sometimes called a *skills audit*) should lead to a
training plan to remedy any deficiencies.

*Language Skills*
Language is the obvious first area to examine. There is no
particular level of proficiency below which language skills
are 'unacceptable': a smattering of any language is likely to
be of some help, even (such is the low level of British

language skills) just showing some willingness to communi-
cate with foreigners (beyond speaking English slowly and
loudly).

Apart from English, French is the main Community
language, in both the Commission and the Council, though
to a lesser extent in the Parliament, and the second language
for many people, particularly Spanish and Portuguese.
Many documents will be available only in French until after
the substantial negotiations are over. French is also widely
spoken in Brussels, Luxembourg and Strasbourg, so making
the logistics of visits easier.

The key skills are, in order of importance:

- Understanding written French (including the technical
  vocabulary of the subject under discussion) so that you
  can read and assimilate documents
- Survival French, for travelling to meetings
- Conversational French, to build up social relationships
  with colleagues and hold discussions in the margins of
  meetings
- Functional French, to contribute in meetings

Other languages are a bonus: German, in particular, is
widely used for technical discussions (while technical
vocabulary in Spanish and Italian can often be puzzled out
from the English and French). Command of any language
also helps in building up an alliance, though language skills
are to be compared to the expectations of the listener: no
French official will be *that* impressed by competent school-
book French, while Finns might be wowed by a few phrases
of their own language (particularly as Finnish has fourteen
declensions!).

*Other Skills*
Many organisations offer training in skills useful in negotiating and lobbying, such as effective presentation and media
handling. They also provide introductions to aspects of the
Community, such as the Structural Funds and the budget,
and cover new developments in areas such as European law.
Although not cheap, such courses can be invaluable in
filling out the skills base of the negotiating team. In addition

to permanent staff, courses usually feature experienced practitioners such as Commission officials. They also provide a chance to exchange experience and best practice with others working on European matters.

The main organisations for short (1–14 day) courses are the Civil Service College, based in London and Sunningdale, the European Centre for Public Affairs at Templeton College, Oxford, and the European Institute for Public Administration in Maastricht. Conference groups and organisations such as the Confederation of British Industry and the Federal Trust run seminars on specific subjects, such as new legislation or the prospects for monetary union.

Contact addresses for those organisations named above are to be found under 'Sources of Further Information' in Appendix III.

## Lobbying Consultants

However good your team, it is always worth considering the merits of bringing in outside help.

Many people look on consultants with great reservations. In part, this is because they are seen as (putting it kindly) poor value. When Brussels was really *terra incognita* for so many business people, some consultants seemed to think it enough just to send their clients extracts from the *Official Journal* (which is to be found in any county library: see Appendix III). The bad old days linger on, though more in the memory than in the reality of modern consulting.

But more than this, people feel, in some vague way, that consultants aren't, or shouldn't be, necessary: that the political process should allow anyone with a good case to get a good hearing (in the same way that you don't *have* to have a barrister if you're being tried for murder at the Old Bailey).

Don't, then, confuse the way things should be with the way things are. This doesn't mean you must employ a consultant, but you will need the skills a consultant should be able to provide. As said before, you need to know the system: if you do not, you should consider bringing such skills on to your team, even if this costs good cold cash.

Consultants should also bring with them contacts. **Access** to the main players in the process is vital: you cannot deploy your winning arguments unless you can actually seat yourself across the desk from the said main player. (See Chapter 14 for more).

What a consultant cannot do, though, is run your campaign for you – even if they say they can. They will not know what your real objectives are, they won't be able to spot hidden dangers or opportunities, they can never understand the subject as well as you; and because at heart they are paid to put over your case, they can never be quite as convincing as you.

> Even among consultants, the saying is, 'The client is his own best advocate.'

So whether or not consultants are part of your negotiating team, if even the other half of a lobbying double-act, there is no escape: you still need to read on, to see how you might plan and implement your negotiating and lobbying strategy.

## Other Sources of Information and Assistance

Whether your team is backed by the full resources of the civil service or a multinational corporation, or whether you are working on a shoestring, you can back up your efforts by building up alliances with other like-minded players (dealt with in the next chapter) and by making use of various sources of information and advice. These are set out in Appendix III, together with contact points and addresses. There are also several key reference works you should have to hand.

## Key Works

Anyone seeking to influence the Brussels system ought to have access to a handful of key works. Most are available from The Stationery Office (the old HMSO) which is also the UK agent for the Official Publications office in Luxembourg. (However, the cost of some might mean you will want to borrow them from your local library.) The Stationery Office address is PO Box 276, London SW8 5DT. Tel: 0171 873 0011 (Enquiries) and 0171 873 9090 (Orders). Fax: 0171 873 8200 (Orders). There are also Stationery Office bookshops in most major UK cities.

You should start with a copy of the Treaty and of the *Directory of European Institutions*, which lists the name and address of all the main policy officials in the Community institutions. Both are available from The Stationery Office or from the Official Publications office in Luxembourg. The Treaty is about 30ecu, the Directory 19ecu (1ecu = about 70p). The European Commission office in London publishes a booklet on *Sources of European Community Funding*, listing most Community spending programmes and including contact points in the Commission and UK Government.

It is also well worth having a recent copy of *Vacher's European Companion* (published quarterly and available from the SO or direct from the publishers). This includes lists of all the MEPs by Committee and by Political Group, and also the staff of the Permanent Representations and the key officials in the Council, Commission and other institutions. It also lists the consultancy firms which specialise in lobbying in Brussels.

Those wishing to work for the European institutions and who are preparing for the entrance competition (*concours*) would find *250 QCM sur l'Europe et la politique européenne* (250 multiple-choice questions) very helpful. It is published by the Syndicat des Fonctionnaires Européens, rue de la Loi 57 (2/44), B-1049 Brussels.

## Other Sources of Information

The *Official Journal of the European Union* (or *OJ*) is published each day and reproduces most documents you will need – texts of Regulations, Directives and Commission proposals, tenders for contracts, announcements of recruitment competitions. The problem is that it is vast, expensive and has no proper index: most of the time, it is better to find the reference elsewhere or buy the particular day's *OJ* that you need.

Various specialist magazines and newsletters follow the EU and its work. Many are very good and provide both facts and some editorial coverage on what is going on now and what might happen in the future. Most are quite expensive and are available only by subscription, but you might ask for a free trial for an issue or two so you can see how useful it would be.

## Further Reading

For a general, academic overview there is *The European Union: Politics and Policies* by John McCormick (Westview/ HarperCollins 1996), which also has the charm of an American perspective. The economics of Europe are dealt with thoroughly in *The Economics of the European Community* by E. M. El-Agraa (Philip Allen 1991) and more digestably in *The Economics of the Single Market* by Dennis Swann (Penguin 1993). For an insight into the heroic early days, there is *Memoirs* by Jean Monnet (Collins 1978) and for a typically breezy view of the Council by Alan Clark's *Diaries*.

If all this gives a taste for more academic or conceptual Euro-studying, there is the *Journal of Common Market Studies* which is published each quarter.

Finally, if you plan to attend a Council working group, Commission conference or plenary session of the European Parliament, make sure you take a good book in case the action slackens a bit. Dickens, Tolstoy, or anything else suitably chunky should do.

# Chapter 12
# Preparing Your Strategy

*The famous Belgian detective twirled his luxuriant moustaches as the suspects, assembled in the library, listened in fascination.*

*'So you see, the murder was planned with great care. The murderer came close to baffling even I, Hercule Pierrot. But now I can reveal who he – or she – is.' He sipped his glass of cassis with relish. 'It was . . . aaarrgh!'*

*Pierrot dropped the glass and collapsed, clutching his throat. The others gathered round, but it was too late. They looked at each other in shock, wondering which of them had prepared this particularly effective negotiating ploy.*

## Introduction

The previous chapter described how the outline of your strategy should emerge from considering the timetable of the negotiation or decision, and also the path it takes through the Brussels maze. Timing is everything: you might know who to lobby, you might know which allies you need in a negotiation: but if you intervene too early or too late, your total impact could be nil.

To start with, you need to gather information; then

arrange it to produce your objectives; then decide how you wish to deploy your resources; and when, where and how to argue your case. Finally, you have to build up alongside your ideal path to victory some alternative routes: either to the same objectives, or to others which may be the best you can reach. In this way, you will be prepared for the unexpected.

## Gathering Information

The point of departure for European negotiations is not only *what are my objectives?* but also *what is being proposed?*

All legislation is, on occasions, complicated or even incomprehensible. European legislation is no exception, and is often written in a style which is ugly and dull (even for bureaucrats), but there is at least a **preamble** at the start of each Directive or Regulation which explains where the proposal has come from and what the legislators thought it was going to do. These recitals, however, point towards a real danger in EU legislation: what legislators intend and what legislation actually means are not always the same.

The gap between intention and result (between intending to legislate on quality standards for bananas only to find you have inadvertently required all farmers to wear hair-nets) comes from a number of sources:

- the complexity of the legislative process
- the way that texts are redrafted by different groups of people (Commission, Council, Parliament) who often do not know why the previous lot used particular wording
- the technical challenge posed by many subjects
- the use of nine languages and national variations
- the desire for difficult decisions to be fudged to help find a compromise

The upshot is: when you receive a proposal, it is worth putting some effort into trying to understand what it means and what the implications would be if applied in its current form. You cannot rely on what it appears to mean, however clear the meaning may seem.

For this, you need legal advice. Beware, though, of asking your friendly local solicitor to take a few hours off from conveyancing and drafting wills to look over a Directive on, say, state aid to the telecoms industry: Community law is a specialist area and it's worth finding an expert, even if the cost rises as a result (which it will).

If you can, bringing in independent legal or expert advice has another key benefit: you cannot rely on what others tell you the legislation means, because:

- they may be wrong
- they may hope it means one thing while in fact it may mean another
- they may be practising upon you the black arts of briefing and lobbying which we will come to later

---

**Trade Associations**

It may be unfair to suggest that trade associations and similar representative bodies are more prone to misleading interpretations of proposals than others (they aren't), but while we know the sorts of axes that political parties, pressure groups and newspapers have to grind, such bodies can seem more impartial.

However, trade associations usually sell a service: providing information and advice to their members, and campaigning on their behalf. (In this, they are similar to lobbying consultants.) They may be tempted to portray new proposals as more dangerous than they are so that those supposedly affected are more likely to pay up their membership fees.

So, if a trade association claims that proposed legislation will put thousands out of jobs, cost millions to implement, and may even cause storms, floods and a plague of frogs, you might consider whether it is ringing alarm bells to drum up custom; and whether a group going in for such antics will best represent your interests in dealing with the power-brokers in London, Brussels or wherever.

## Consultation

Consulting others – business and industry, local authorities, charities and non-governmental organisations, and individuals – is a vital part of proper preparation. Devising your strategy in a vacuum, without knowing the views of others, is unlikely to result in a suitably balanced and realistic position. The point of consultation is two-fold: to **explain** the implications of proposals and options; and to **canvass** views on them to help formulate your position. Clearly, the two form a continuous, circular process.

Consultation should start when a new proposal is envisaged. It would draw on existing networks, but you will need to:

- identify who needs to be consulted
- consider what the consultees will want from the process
- establish the necessary procedures, being realistic about available resources

As with consultation across Whitehall (see Chapter 9), simply sending out a proposal from the Commission with a covering letter is not enough, and is likely to prove counterproductive: such proposals are usually impossible to comprehend on first reading, and the resulting ignorance will breed uncertainty or even fear. Hostile forces, be they journalists looking for a 'good' anti-EU story, or trade associations boosting themselves by building up the 'threat from Brussels' which only they can resist, will make full use of this.

---

**The COM-DOC and the Canary**

The Commission's 1992 proposed Wildlife Trade Regulation hid a ticking time-bomb: Article 4 proposed to limit the taking of birds such as falcons from the wild by requiring all owners of species of native birds to have a licence.

Now the Canary Islands are a part of the Community, and canaries are native to the Canary Islands. The DOE team realised that, if they weren't careful, the tabloid

> press would have a field day: 'Brussels Loonycrats
> Ban Canaries'; 'Jacques Delors Ate My Budgie'; and so
> on.
>    So the team took great care to reassure consultees
> that they had taken the point and would fight to get
> this anomaly resolved. The consultees therefore did
> not whip up the press or launch a national campaign.
> The point was quietly dealt with in working group, and
> millions of canary-owners (and civil servants) were
> saved from unnecessary worry.

Therefore the **implications** of proposals should be explained
as far as possible, as should the negotiation process, so that
those hearing of proposals do not think that they are about
to have their lives turned upside down. The difference
between a Commission proposal and a Council Directive is
often lost on civil servants, let alone the ordinary citizen, to
whom all forms of administration are duller than ditch-
water and more impenetrable than quantum mechanics.
Consultation documents should therefore explain:

- what is being proposed
- the likely timetable for negotiations
- the scope for amendments (i.e., don't panic)
- how to make views known
- what else consultees can do, including lobbying the EU
  institutions

This implies a mini-version of this guide: here is one
already prepared for use within Whitehall and which could
be tailored to your specific consultation exercises.

> ### A Consultation Paper for All Occasions
>
> *Introduction*
> This is a proposal from the **European Commission** to
> regulate the production of toadstools. The final form of
> legislation will be determined by the **Council**, made up
> of Ministers from each Member State, in co-operation
> with the European Parliament.
>    There is every chance for you to influence the
> outcome of the legislation. Your views will be taken

into account in drawing up the UK's negotiating position. You may also lobby other Member States, the Commission and the European Parliament directly or through domestic or European trade associations. **But you need to act quickly**: the pace of European negotiations is difficult to predict, and in any case views tend to carry more weight in the early stages.

*The Meaning of the Proposal*
The Department has drawn up an initial assessment of what the proposal from the Commission means for toadstool-growers and others with an interest: industry, consumer protection and environmental groups, and others. This is attached. You are invited to a meeting at the Department on 1 April to discuss this paper. This will be a first chance for you to put over your views and meet the negotiating team. If you would like to attend, please contact . . .

Some elements of the proposal may be worrying to you and you may see coverage in the media which paints a yet more alarming picture. You should remember that the Commission text is only a proposal for discussion. While there is a risk these elements may not be resolved in negotiations, the chances are that they will, particularly if you take steps now to alert us to the problems. In short, **don't panic but do act**.

*Likely Timing*
We expect negotiations to start on 1 June and to last between twelve and eighteen months. The European Parliament is likely to draw up its position in the early autumn. The Commission would then re-examine its proposal and may suggest further amendments.

The final Directive is likely to allow two or three years for each Member State to transpose it into their national law. Some specific provisions in the proposal may be phased in later than that.

*Next Steps*
You can write to the Department now or after the 1 April meeting. You might also:

● Alert colleagues in other Member States: they may

not yet be aware of the proposals and may share your concerns. Pressure co-ordinated across Europe will be much more effective than from one Member State alone.

- Write to your MEP, particularly if there is a strong constituency interest such as widespread toadstool production.
- Contact a trade association or umbrella group, such as the British Mushroom and Toadstool Federation; the European equivalent, EuroStool; or the pressure group Mushpeace.

*Lobbying*

Your lobbying effort will be most effective if you explain exactly what the problem is with the proposal; and also suggest ways in which it can be avoided (ideally without just arguing for an exemption). For example, if you think small-scale producers are being included even though they do not cause an environmental problem, it will probably be more effective to submit any evidence you have and suggest an improved definition of 'producer' rather than say the whole proposal should be scrapped. **Suggest solutions as well as raising problems**: that way the solutions are more likely to meet your needs.

## Setting Objectives

Objectives always vary depending on who you are and what the subject is, but there is one key point to bear in mind: you have to be realistic in your aims and prepared to be flexible in securing as many of them as possible. This may mean moving closer to the objectives of others as part of the process of building up an alliance which will be more powerful – and have more chance of success – than when operating alone. It may mean changing direction, if you realise that your current course will take you nowhere, or where a better avenue opens up which will secure more of your aims.

One note of warning, though: you need also to revisit your objectives as time passes, to avoid the risk of forgetting your most fundamental aims. This is particularly important when you are taking an initiative or have put a great deal of financial, physical or emotional capital into a project, be it a new Directive or a project which requires Community funding. Changing direction, admitting that so much effort has been wasted, even killing a proposal which you conceived and nurtured, can be terrible moments (see box), but the decisions need to be faced.

---

**Cautionary Tales**
There are many examples from the arts of the difficulties of destroying your own projects. Remember Dr Frankenstein's cry of anguish? (*'It is a monster that I have created, an abomination! But I cannot destroy it!'*) Or Alec Guinness as the British officer refusing to blow up the bridge on the River Kwai. (*'Dammit! We built the bloody thing!'*)

---

## Creating Alliances

Alliances are based on shared concerns and shared objectives. Where two or more parties to a negotiation share enough common ground, they can agree to pool their efforts and work towards an agreed programme. This is distinct from happening to have the same aims (without co-ordination) or from occasionally pushing the same line (as you might if briefing a journalist to air your concerns). Alliances are active, usually on-going, and always have responsibilities as well as benefits.

Alliances often emerge from negotiations, but they might also be predicted from prior experience of the positions taken by others, and sometimes such 'like-minded' groups live on: in overseas aid, for example, the Netherlands, Germany, Denmark and the UK were for years known as the 'Northern Quadrilateral' because of their four-way co-ordination prior to major meetings (the name was ruined by the accession of more northern Member States).

Once potential allies have been spotted, a bilateral meeting to 'talk over' the issues should rapidly expose common ground: they, like you, should want mutual support. Then comes the difficult negotiation: what shape does the alliance take? For, except in rare cases where your interests are identical, you are likely to want their support on points which, in fact, are of little or no interest to them: they, naturally, will want the same in return. So alliance-building means concentrating on a group of shared objectives (which will include points included to satisfy only one side) and avoiding doing the other side down on other points.

Alliances, then, require commitments, and you should not enter into them unless you are fairly sure you can deliver what you have promised. The key to alliances is trust, and failing to perform will kill that trust, damage your own credibility and make other alliances much harder to put together in the future. It is rare to find a negotiation, let alone a negotiating point, so vital that it is worth risking your credibility in this way (though this does not mean that you should not consider whether you might be the *victim* of such untrustworthiness: it is always worth having a contingency plan).

Trust plays a key role, in part because it is very rare for two unconnected points to be settled at the same time during a negotiation. A deal which swapped support for an exemption from the Catering Directive for cream teas in return for similar help on food served in beer gardens might come apart if the two points were not agreed at the same meeting. Keeping both sides of such alliances together is more difficult once one side has what it wanted.

**Dumping the Alliance**

In 1990 the Commission proposed a Directive setting standards for landfill (waste disposal) sites. This Landfill Directive was unpopular with several Member States: notably Spain, Italy, Greece, Ireland and the UK. Together, this would-be alliance had more than enough votes to block the proposal and extract concessions.

The supporters of the Directive therefore went to

work, offering special terms to areas of sparse population (which helped Spain); mountainous areas (which
helped Spain and Italy); and to small islands (which
helped Greece a great deal). As the opposition melted
away, the UK and Ireland saw the hole opening in front
of them and changed tack to extract helpful concessions of their own.

(In the event, the proposal was lost in the Parliament, and all now wait with trepidation for Landfill II.)

Finally, any alliance is most likely to go wrong – or be less
effective – where communication breaks down. Never take
the other parties for granted, and keep them informed.
Particularly, make sure you co-ordinate positions ahead of
significant meetings.

## Ensuring Coherence

Your strategy needs to cover not only your own actions, but
also those of your allies and of other players. All moves to
influence the outcome will have more impact if properly co-
ordinated, in terms of both the action and the timing.
Communication within your organisation and within your
alliance is vital: you should be making the same or similar
points, should ensure lobbying is timed properly, and that
effort is not duplicated. Not only does this waste time and
resources, but unco-ordinated briefing or lobbying can result
in the recipients becoming deeply unimpressed with your
organisation and, by extension, your arguments.

Remember too that your action will have a ripple effect:
what you say will be passed on, and others may react by
lobbying or briefing of their own. If you start on a new
campaign, this may precipitate others to do the same,
which, in turn, could affect your chances of success.

These ripples also mean you must avoid speaking with a
forked tongue: you can tailor your message to suit your
audience when you brief or lobby – indeed, you must do to
some extent to be effective – but you cannot take this as far
as seeming to hold contradictory positions. Telling one

audience that you support a proposal and another that you are against is asking for trouble. In most negotiations, little can be hidden, and however subtle you might think you have been, the secrets may seep out. As before, influencing should not be about misleading people: trustworthiness is valuable and virtually impossible to recover once lost.

## Influencing Proposals at the Formative Stage

An essential principle is that the earlier you get your views across, the more chance you have of influencing the debate. As the Commission is where legislative proposals come from, you should try to keep abreast of thinking about future work and the initial preparation of proposals. Following the specialist press is of some help, but direct contacts with Commission officials are much more effective, not least because you can put your views across at the same time.

For government officials, the meetings of national experts often held before the Commission formally adopts a proposal provide a chance to build up personal contacts with colleagues from other Member States: these are **absolutely vital** (much more so than in the UK system) and should be cultivated whenever possible to help your negotiating effort.

Weaving a web of contacts shouldn't be a chore: colleagues in other administrations are as likely to understand your concerns as anyone in Whitehall, and are, in the main, perfectly pleasant people. Buying drinks in the bar is a start; more personal gestures are ideal. If one of your colleagues expresses undying affection for *Fawlty Towers*, see if you can find a tape to lend them; or if it's for Marmite, bring a jar to the next meeting. This is not a matter of calculation or bribery, but allowing natural human friendliness into the workplace.

On a practical level, your colleagues and opposite numbers often face the same problems you do, so it's well worth comparing notes with them. Their experiences may help clarify your own thinking. Such basic exchanges can establish a commonality of interest, itself the foundation for building effective and resilient alliances. Seize any opportunities for bilaterals, either in the margins of meetings in

Brussels or in their capitals. Sprinkle some invites to London too (perhaps timed to coincide with the sales as an added attraction).

The same considerations apply to Commission officials. They too are often under-resourced and short of practical information. Providing ideas and possible approaches to shared concerns will almost always be welcome. One key move at this early stage is to explain your position clearly, on paper and perhaps in a meeting. A large part of lobbying is not changing people's minds, but filling them.

One area to concentrate on is explaining sector-specific and national practices. This is crucial: there is a world of difference between variations and derogations. Variations deliver the flexibility necessary to legislate for a Union of fifteen nations and 350 million citizens: derogations, on the other hand, are concessions to individual Member States designed to win their agreement to an unpalatable package. In terms of the effort required to secure them, variations are much cheaper than derogations.

When the Commission starts to sketch out on a blank sheet of paper its plans for new legislation, everything is possible. By explaining national practices – or even particular methods used by a specific sector or an individual factory – your concerns, or at least some flexibility, can be built in from the start.

---

### Peas in Our Time

Were the Commission to be asked to draft a Directive on quality standards for garden peas, it might well specify a certain level of greenness. But if from the start the Commission is made aware of British tastes, the definition of peas might be drafted to include only garden peas, so leaving the Great Grey British Mushy Pea unmolested.

However, if the Commission drafts or, even worse, adopts a Directive with a wider definition, this would need the agreement of the Commission, other Member States and the Parliament to change the definition or give the UK a derogation. While this may well be possible, it is bound to use valuable negotiating capital

> you would rather use elsewhere, such as resisting a pea firmness criteria and so avoiding the inevitable 'Brussels Squashes the British Pea' headlines.

At this early stage, officials usually consider with colleagues whether the subject is important enough to justify offering a secondee to the Commission (ideally as a Detached National Expert). The Commission welcomes the assistance secondees provide and UK officials are well respected (although there are often resource and bureaucratic hurdles to clear). In return, the department benefits from having an official working on a proposal who understands the UK and in particular its administrative system.

Proposals are easier to mould into an acceptable shape before adoption by the Commission. This is the moment to intervene, initially at working level. If the draft proposal poses serious problems, or suggestions for improvements are not well received, these might be raised with senior Commission officials or with Commissioners.

Once a proposal has been cleared within the Directorate-General, it goes to cabinets and to the College of Commissioners. At this point friendly (British and other) cabinets may ask through UKRep for background information on the proposal and the positions of individual Member States. Though such requests often come at short notice, the results from briefing fully are worth the trouble: cabinets and Commissioners can insist on substantial changes to proposals or even return them to DGs for complete revision. They may also press for the rapid adoption of proposals.

If such requests do not materialise, you may wish to provide the information in any case. Commissioners or their staff will usually hear out a concerned party: the key is to make you pitch to the right person. Here, you have to be realistic: Commissioners are busy people with wide responsibilities, and your approach should recognise this. Take note of the points in Chapter 15 and, assuming your initial approach is on paper:

- set out the background as succinctly as possible
- explain why the problem matters to you and others
- say what you want the Commissioner to do

The last of these is the trickiest, as you have to think like a bureaucrat (sometimes difficult, even if you are one) to be able to suggest solutions which the bureaucratic machine can deliver. Realistic ways of solving problems will always be better received than a maximalist demand which is not politically practical. The College of Commissioners works by consensus, and individual Commissioners take an oath not to favour a specific Member State, so saying 'Vote against the adoption of Proposal X – it's bad for Britain' is unrealistic. However, saying 'The proposal is burdensome – ask for an amendment to exclude factories employing fewer than ten people' is much more realistic, as it would match the Commission's stated policies to avoid overregulation, promote competitiveness, and support small and medium enterprises.

## Negotiating

Negotiating lies at the heart of any influencing strategy. Negotiating in the EU is covered in Chapter 13 but in terms of preparing your strategy, two key points should be remembered:

- The timetable is set by others (the Presidency, the Commission, or business managers in the Parliament) and by the legislative process.
- Most of the time, you will need the support of others to secure your objectives, whatever the voting system. Qualified Majority Voting requires alliances to avoid isolation, while even the use of the veto is likely to bring negative effects and spill over into other policy areas unless others have some sympathy with your position.

## Lobbying

The first thing to say about lobbying in Brussels is 'It's OK: everyone's at it.' All the politicians and officials you are likely to meet will be used to lobbying and on the whole fairly open to approaches from officials of Member State administrations and other interested parties. The most serious constraint on *access* to them is usually pressure of time (though other considerations such as political sensitivities play a role too). In any case, meetings should ideally have a clear **purpose** and offer something to those being lobbied as well. Chapter 14 covers this in more detail.

## Briefing

Briefing, whether written and oral, and whether for use within your organisation or sent to others, needs to be tailored to take account of:

- the user
- the audience
- where it is to be used or distributed

Your strategy in preparing and deploying outside briefing needs to consider the choice of media for putting over your message; 'piggy-backing' on briefing and other material put out by others, including briefing the media to try to put over your points; and briefing at one remove (where you provide the information for others to use).

## Logistics

Finally, your strategy cannot exist in a vacuum: it must take account of the physical realities of working in Europe. Chapter 16 provides a guide for those attending meetings or visiting Brussels, Luxembourg and Strasbourg to lobby or just see how it all works at first hand. Your strategy needs to build in the costs, time constraints, even the difficulties of finding a meeting room near the Parliament building in Strasbourg during the plenary. It's no use having prepared the best presentation of your case for MEPs – with overhead slides and marble jam-pot paperweights as mementoes – if you have to hold your meeting in a car park.

# Chapter 13
# Negotiations

*Midnight in Dodge City, when the stakes are high and the drinks are cheap in the Lipsius Saloon. In the back room there's no movement but for seventeen pairs of eyes shifting rapidly from seventeen hands of cards to the other sixteen faces ranged around the table. A haze of smoke fills the room.*

*'OK, Limey. I match yer two. An' I raise yer two.'*

*There's a stir, a thrill of anticipation through the crowd. Hands move towards six-shooters. And all eyes switch to you.*

*But you're bluffing. All you have in your hand is a pair of threes and a briefing note on subsidiarity. Your move . . .*

## Introduction

Negotiations in the Union demand effective and thorough **preparation**, tempered by **flexibility** once the talking starts. Achieving your negotiating goals is easiest when other Member States share the same objectives or concerns: if they don't, try to explain your stance and create some unease.

You may be able to use brilliant oratory and negotiating skills to win over converts or reduce opposition. But if this is not enough, you come down to horse-trading, where you have to know what everyone wants and what price they will pay to gain it.

Proposals being developed within the Commission can be influenced by timely lobbying, and the same approach can build up an alliance of those sharing some or all of your objectives. Such alliance-building often shades into negotiation: putting together 'You scratch my back I'll scratch yours' deals can require considerable negotiating skills.

Nevertheless, it is when the proposal moves out of the Commission that the complexity of Community negotiations becomes clear, as fifteen Member States and the Commission begin their discussions, the Parliament waits in the wings, and industry, pressure groups and the rest cluster outside the door.

This chapter is therefore addressed to the officials who negotiate within the Council structures, but it should also give those outside an insight into the process and how they might go about influencing the outcome.


## Negotiations in the Council

*Council Documents*

The Council is where the Member States reach agreement on proposals from the Commission. This is done on the basis of a document prepared by the Committee of Permanent Representatives, which in turn is prepared by the appropriate working group. This document consists of two parts: a revised version of the text of the Directive or Regulation itself, and a series of footnotes detailing the alternative positions of the Member States and the Commission.

This demonstrates the two tasks which the Council gives to Coreper and its working groups: to **revise the text** of the proposal, and to **prepare those questions** which cannot be resolved by officials for discussion and decision by Ministers. Naturally, this influences the pace of negotiations and also the type of point which can be raised at each stage.

Ministers in Council hate redrafting. Rewriting legislation, coming up with new formulations in a Council
meeting itself, is not only difficult for Ministers, who
inevitably are not experts on the details of a proposal, but is
also dangerous: there are only very limited opportunities, in
a Council lasting one or two days, for considering in full the
implications of particular wording, or for consulting interested parties. Further, what might appear on the surface to
be an elegant solution to a tricky problem might, once
scrutinised at leisure by the lawyers, be shown to have nasty
side-effects.

The footnotes which accompany the revised text usually
try to minimise this problem by setting out the alternative
wording which each Member State or group of states wishes
to see. In this way, the implications of these options can be
assessed beforehand. The Presidency will also try to ensure
that problems of a kind which cannot be presented in this
way are dealt with before the Council.

Therefore, a typical dossier passed to Council by Coreper
might have three remaining questions: the **scope** of the
legislation, for example in terms of the product groups it
covers; the **date** of entry into force of the various provisions;
and the **derogations** allowed to certain Member States.
While the arguments behind all these questions might well
be complex, the *means* of resolving them are more straightforward: dates are set; product groups included or excluded;
derogations for specific circumstances (such as the traditional low cocoa content of British chocolate) allowed.

Sometimes a compromise text has to be produced during
the Council by the Presidency or the Commission, or by one
or more Member States. This leads to a flurry of hurried
conferences between experts, lawyers, diplomats and Ministers around the Council chamber or in the corridors outside,
from which emerges agreement (or otherwise). But in many
cases, the wording to be included in the final text agreed
under the common position will be exactly the same as one
or other of the options set out in the paper from Coreper to
Council.

So, when the working group begins to discuss a new
proposal from the Commission, the objective of the delegation is not only to have the text of the proposal amended in

specific ways, but also to handle the negotiations so that, when the crunch comes, the Minister and his or her delegation can do as well as possible in the final settlement.

## Working Groups

The start of negotiations in the Council working groups is a good time to reassess your negotiating position and the likelihood of securing each of your objectives. For government negotiators, a meeting of the team working on the proposal is a must, bringing in others with an interest as appropriate to ensure all parties are fully engaged and to contribute to and comment on the written instructions (in effect a negotiating brief) for the UK Representation in Brussels.

Most working groups are made up of attachés from the Permanent Representations, supported by experts from capitals, depending on the subject under discussion. The main ones meet on one or two days each week, and so the attachés know each other well and can discuss issues and put together alliances in an atmosphere of trust. Attachés also see the overlap between dossiers and the links to horizontal issues such as Community competence, and are adept at drafting around particular problems. They are also the best way into the Presidency team in Brussels, complementing the links which departmental co-ordinators have to the Presidency team in the home capital.

Attachés are not, however, experts on each subject, and so each delegation acts as a team. Attachés usually speak, briefed by their experts, on the basis that if the expert cannot explain a point succinctly to his own attaché he will never be able to explain it to eight interpreters and fifteen other delegations. However, it is often useful for experts to speak as well, so that they can gain experience and put over complex (particularly scientific or legal) points authoritatively.

## Coreper

Negotiations in the Committee of Permanent Representatives follow much the same pattern, but at a more high-powered level. Officials from capitals do not attend: the

Ambassador or Deputy Ambassador is advised by the relevant attachés. Most of the time, Coreper only considers dossiers which are about to go to Council and operates under great pressure. Not only does each Coreper have a vast amount of business to get through in preparing perhaps ten dossiers for a single Council meeting, but it may also have to prepare several Councils in a single week. This is most likely to happen towards the end of a Presidency, in June and late November/early December. Worst of all, the Ambassadors and Deputies also have to attend these Councils themselves, to advise or stand in for Ministers.

So the Ambassadors and Deputies in Coreper tend to come to dossiers under three constraints:

- The issues are often unfamiliar
- The Council is only a few days away
- Other subjects have to be dealt with too

In this light, it should be easy to imagine the reaction to a Member State raising a new concern at the last moment or showing an unwillingness to accept a reasonable compromise. Much better, whenever possible, to resolve issues long before Coreper. This said, Coreper can be most effective at problem-solving, as it comes to issues with a fresh eye and a sense of proportion. Were it to have a motto, it might be 'The best is the enemy of the good.'

If Coreper judges that the dossier is not yet ready for Ministers to consider, it may pressure the Presidency to either:

- reconvene the working group to continue negotiations and report back to the next Coreper meeting;
- hold an orientation debate in Council, rather than trying to press for a common position; or
- drop the item from the Council agenda altogether

*Council*
At Council, officials advise Ministers orally and on paper (see Chapter 15), and both conduct mini-negotiations with their opposite numbers in the margins (known as *corridor*

*diplomacy*: see below). The key differences between Council and the preparatory committees are that Member States can only pursue a very limited number of objectives and, without support from others, will be hard placed to gain concessions; and that errors usually cannot be rectified later.

Points of detail or drafting may be referred by Council to a **parallel working group**: this works in a similar way to the normal group, except that attachés may not be present throughout; and the group works to a deadline for reporting back to the Council (which continues to consider other agenda items) so that the pressure to find a resolution is intense.

## Commission Working Groups

Negotiating in the various committees and working parties set up to advise the Commission and to implement, monitor and update legislation is reassuringly similar to Council working groups. The main differences are:

- The Commission chairs the meeting (rather than the Presidency) and prepares the agenda, minutes and other papers (rather than the Council secretariat).
- Attachés rarely attend, and the committees do not report to Coreper.
- The various committee procedures (rather than the legislative processes detailed in Article 189 of the Treaty) apply, so determining the respective powers of the Member States and the Commission.
- The style of each committee varies much more than between Council working groups, and they also have varying formal and informal working methods.

The UK position for Commission working groups should be thought through and expressed just as carefully as for a Council working group, including tactics and fall-backs. As part of the team-working approach, colleagues in UKRep and elsewhere are copied in on notes of meetings and papers on the dossier in general, so that they are better able to offer advice. For more on the conduct of Commission-chaired meetings, see Chapter 5.

# Negotiating

Chapter 11 explained how negotiations have a rhythm or pattern: the first task of a negotiator is to tune into that pattern. Here are three concepts which may help: negotiating capital; timing; and slipstreaming.

*Negotiating Capital*
In the Community, there is an unstated assumption that each delegation may raise a certain number of points or objections: what might be thought of as its store of good-will or **negotiating capital**. The flip-side of this is that those delegations raising more points or insisting on more changes **will not win all their points, however much they make sense**. This may not be fair, but it is reality, and the UK is at particular risk of suffering from *intervention fatigue* because its officials are usually quick to spot the flaws in the text of a proposal.

> **Intervention Fatigue**
> This term describes the feeling of one delegation that another is speaking too much, or asking for too much: *Oh no, here we go again, what do they want this time?* Intervention fatigue leads to other delegations switching off mentally (paying less attention to each point) and, at its worst, even physically: other delegations switch off the simultaneous translation headsets, chat about their own positions, go and speak to other delegates or start reading the *FT*. Every working group seems to have the official whose interventions coincide with other delegates going out for a coffee, secure in the knowledge that, twenty minutes later, they can return without having missed anything of importance.
>   Don't let it be you!

The practical lessons to learn are that you must always have a clear sense of the importance of a particular point – there is no real benefit in winning some minor textual change if you lose the main prize as a result – and also be prepared to let points go. This may be the harder of the two lessons, but sometimes when you believe, or even *know* you are right, you will not win the necessary support. In such circumstances, there comes a time when there is no benefit in pressing a point, and where carrying on becomes counter-productive. In any case, there may be a chance to retrieve the point later on. This leads to the second concept:

*Timing*
Negotiations are rarely conducted in a day, so settle in for the long haul. There is usually no need to argue every point at the first read-through of the proposal: these can be brought up later on, hopefully by another delegation which you can then judiciously support in a brief intervention. The text under negotiation will always have points in it which you want changed, but this takes time: they have to be picked off one by one rather than in some sort of big bang.

Timing also determines the most favourable moment for raising concerns. As said above, technical and drafting points are ill-suited to discussion in Coreper and Council, even if they might have a significant impact when the legislation is enacted. So, when considering whether texts offered in working group or Coreper are acceptable, think about your chances of a successful debate in the Council.

If taking a point to Council cannot be avoided, you also need to consider how it is presented in the paper to Council from Coreper. Talk to the Presidency to ensure that the wording you favour is included as an option, and wherever possible get other Member States to indicate that they could agree to your option (even if they are neutral).

A final thought on timing: a typical negotiation is a long-distance race, but it does speed up markedly towards the end. Minor points will be swept aside, so it is vital before a dossier begins its final preparation for Council to **refocus** on **real and achievable priorities** at the start of the end-game. The Presidency should signal quite clearly when they think a dossier is ready for Council to try and reach a common position: this is a good time to look (and be) constructive. You might, with a flourish, drop some minor points in return for concessions from others or even just some intangible good-will: in a few days or weeks, you will have to drop the points anyway to concentrate on your main concerns.

*Slipstreaming*
Throughout the negotiations, you should resist the temptation to lead the attack on all occasions: the UK often leads with the chin and others make use of this. Turn the tables and **slipstream** other delegations. When others look at the UK delegation expecting a complaint about competence or subsidiarity, smile back and say nothing: they will then have to break cover and make the point themselves. Slipstreaming saves valuable negotiating capital for the UK: at the same time, it forces other delegations to take up a public position of support from which it is less easy for them to retreat.

## Making Your Case

The need for focus applies to each individual point you make: don't dilute a good case with weak subsidiary arguments. Remember that, to pass effectively through simultaneous translation and convince other delegations, an argument has to be clear. At the same time, consider the **relative priorities** of the points you wish to make. You may judge it more important to secure agreement to a single key point at a particular stage rather than to several minor ones.

## Speaking in Meetings

Most formal meetings in Brussels are provided with interpretation (simultaneous translation) into most (but rarely all) Community languages. Speakers use microphones, and those listening in other languages use the earphones provided at each seat. The system soon becomes familiar, but there are rules to follow to ensure that users make the most of it.

Firstly, it is the President who decides who speaks when, usually from a list noted down by the Council Secretariat, so catch the eye of the Council Secretariat official as well as waving a pencil (waving of national name-plates is not done). There is no fixed rule about when it is best to speak (see box): use the firm early intervention to set the terms of the debate, the quiet intervention mid-round, or the masterly summing-up once others have opined, as appropriate. But whatever you do, **don't go on and on, and don't ask to speak too often!**

Otherwise, the best interventions are those which:

- are measured, clear and concise
- put over a small number of points (no minor sub-arguments which cloud the issue)
- have a recognisable structure (so that others can follow the logic of the argument: this is a characteristically French approach which others will recognise or even expect)
- avoid English colloquialisms
- use humour when appropriate (but not irony, colloquial humour or word-play, and definitely *not* jokes made at the expense of friends on the continent)
- enumerate and recapitulate your key points

---

**When to Speak**
The timing of interventions can matter, so get in early if you want to . . .

- steer the debate along particular lines
- convince waverers
- head off counter-proposals or spoil someone else's intervention
- set out some important material considerations
- support the Presidency's compromise proposal

Come in late if you . . .

- think others will make your points for you
- want to hear the arguments of others first so you can counter them

---

- think you may pick up something intelligent from another delegation
- want to be Presidential by summarising the debate and drawing conclusions

If your intervention will help the Presidency to reach agreement, tell them before the point comes up. They can then call on you to speak at the right time. This is very effective at Council, where the first Minister to speak often sets the tone. Talk to UKRep, who can set this up with the Presidency.

Sometimes, other delegations chat away so much during interventions that your points might be lost. If the Presidency doesn't come to your rescue, a pause while others remember their manners should do the trick. Ploughing on with no one listening is pointless (and faintly embarrassing).

**It's For You . . .**
One UK official at a working group was interrupted in mid-intervention by a sinister bleeping. He struggled on, but the noise was clearly coming from his delegation. Sheepishly, he had to leave the room to take a call on his mobile phone. On his return, the performance was repeated, with 'I'm in a meeting. Can I call you back?' being picked up by the microphone and translated into seven other languages.

The following week, signs sprouted over the building saying 'No Mobile Phones in Meeting Rooms', thus showing that Britain really can make an impact in Europe.

Effective negotiating requires good **listening skills**. Interventions from others are not there to allow you time to polish your next telling piece of oratory: they pass on concrete information and usually have hidden signals about possible compromises and real sticking-points. Once you know what each of the other delegations is really looking for, then you are better placed to put forward packages and compromises which will gain widespread support. Naturally, listening to their interventions in the original language is the best approach of all, as you gain more of the tone and nuance.

---

**Interpretation**
The simultaneous translation service provided by the interpreters is usually very good, but there are times when points don't come over clearly. If possible, one of your delegation should try to listen to as much as possible in another language to check the message is getting through.

Or you could try to emulate a former UK Deputy Permanent Representative, who used to sit in Coreper monitoring how his interventions were being translated in French *while he was still speaking!*

---

This will also help you to **anticipate** the arguments of others so that you can prepare for them and, ideally, rebut them. You might also play on inconsistencies or contradictions in their positions, either across dossiers or even within single proposals. One way of doing this is to keep a very full note of each meeting and, much like a policeman's notebook, occasionally quote previous statements back at delegations, to their discomfort. The Commission is particularly vulnerable, and the explanatory memorandum which they produce to accompany each proposal can be a rich source of quotes.

## Written Submissions

Circulating suggested amendments on paper as well as orally usually increases their persuasiveness: ideally, these should follow a clear format (see box). You may even be able to offer your impartial linguistic skills to help the Presidency draft a compromise in English. If done with subtlety, UK concerns can be met in a text with a Presidency label.

---

**Toadstools Directive**

Suggested Amendments from the UK Delegation:
1 April 1996

Article 4
Member States shall ensure that, in all proposed amendments, <u>changes to the text are
underlined</u>, the text is properly spaced out;
and omissions from the text [. . .] are marked
by square brackets and three dots.

---

The text should be typed, sufficient copies for each delegation printed, and circulated **before** the point is discussed.
Usually the *huissiers* (the Council Secretariat staff who
manage the meeting rooms) will copy and circulate any
papers passed to the Council Secretariat representative on
the group, but this takes time (allow twenty minutes).
Another approach is to group all proposed amendments into
a single document, to be circulated to delegations **before** the
meeting, allowing time for consideration and for the UK to
whip up some support amongst other Member States.

---

**IPPC**
The draft Integrated Pollution Prevention and Control
Directive contained an annex listing the hundred or
more industries to be covered. One entry used the term
'melting' to describe certain forms of metal processing:
the correct term would have been 'smelting'. This was
spotted and pointed out by the UK delegation on a
number of occasions, with no success. Others listened
politely, nodded their agreement, but each successive
text retained the word 'melting'. This was no con-
spiracy, just an extreme example of how the process
can ignore points which somehow fail to capture the
interest of other groups. Once this happens, repetition
by a single delegation can just be wasted breath.

## The Margins

Remember that the meeting doesn't end when you leave the table. Discussions in coffee bars, over lunch or in the margins of the meeting can be crucial, and give an opportunity to float ideas and possible compromises informally. These forms of *corridor diplomacy* come to the fore at Council: there you should keep looking about for any covert meetings or huddles of officials, try to muscle in and then report back. Those including the Presidency, Commission or Council Secretariat would have priority. Identify the key players and ensure you sit next to them at lunch (but don't bilge on about the dossier if they'd rather have an hour off and talk about the latest Lars von Trier film). Finally, gaining sight (or even copies) of texts under discussion before they have been formally released earns maximum credit.

## Positioning and Alliance-Building

Remember that most legislation is agreed by Qualified Majority Voting: no one has a veto. This is crucial to any strategy, because a Presidency will look for a qualified majority, and the best place to be while it does so will often be **on the margin** of the QM. Those in outright opposition will be discounted: those firmly inside the majority will be taken for granted; it is those in between who will be courted and offered concessions by the Presidency and others to come aboard the majority position.

This is not the only option, however. Sometimes you may need to oppose outright, and the best way to rally others to your flag is to be seen to be firm. Alternatively, you may wish to take part in the majority-building: that is, to work out with other delegations a package that meets the main UK objectives which the others agree to protect in return for UK adherence to the package as a whole.

The choice of strategy depends on the individual circumstances of each dossier. What always remains true is that one must weigh up the options; make a firm choice of strategy; but remain ready to change it (though not too often:

those who keep changing tack will be abandoned by other delegations as too unreliable to do deals with).

## Day-to-Day Considerations

Review your alliances and tactics as necessary. Nurture your personal contacts. Assess the strength of others and keep alongside/butter up the Commission, the Presidency, the *next* Presidency and the Council Secretariat where possible.

Make time to discuss the issues and progress so far in person with UKRep before each meeting of the working group. Consider with them the scope for tabling new drafting suggestions or ideas which might form part of Presidency compromises.

Bear in mind that apparent problems may arise from inaccurate translation. Where possible, compare the English text with other languages.

Make sure you understand the difference between the various types of implementing committee (regulatory, management or advisory) to be established under a Directive or Regulation (*comitology*). Some of the committees leave considerable power to implement legislation in the hands of the Commission, and the best committee for the UK will not always be a Type IIIb: this needs tactical judgement as well (see Chapter 5).

Keep interested parties informed of progress through your consultation machinery (see Chapter 11) but remember that Council documents themselves should not in principle be circulated outside government. Where other departments have an interest, it may be necessary to resolve any differences through Cabinet Office machinery, so keep the Cabinet Office European Secretariat aware of the main issues and any likely disputes, and try to leave time to resolve any inter-departmental disputes before Council.

---

**Covert Operations**
Meetings can be very friendly and informal: but don't drop your guard. The threat comes less from other Member States than from outside groups. After one

international meeting, representatives from a certain campaigning group were found going through the waste-paper baskets looking for incriminating evidence on the positions of other delegations.

## Tips on Negotiating

In many ways, negotiating in the Union is like playing bridge with sixteen players: there is the same assessment of your own hand, some calculation of what others must have, and then a judgement over what you are likely to win. It also, though, has the flavour of poker, particularly in the psychology. So, some final thoughts on negotiations as an (unspecified) game of cards:

**Keep a poker face**. Negotiations have a natural, unspoken balance, and the search for compromise is supposed to avoid 'winners' and 'losers'. If a point made and secured by another delegation helps the UK, don't show this in a meeting by smiling or thanking that delegation: better to pocket the advantage without comment of any sort and continue to pursue other points. Others will assume you still need to be 'given' something to balance the deal.

**Don't overbid**. The best gamblers walk away from the table when they are ahead. Try to avoid risking good-will, or even worse the substantial concessions you have already won, by pursuing minor points. You could lose the lot.

**Don't fold too soon**. There can be great pressure to deliver a deal, and not doing so is often seen as failure, but it may be better to hold on for the right package. You may not always be able to stop a proposal being agreed (remember it's almost all Qualified Majority Voting), but don't agree for the sake of it.

**Never deal from the bottom of the pack.** Negotiations give the chance for double-dealing and other tricks, but beware. If you deliberately mislead another delegation or renege on a deal, they will take it personally and do all in their power to take revenge on you and the UK as a whole. **The best asset anyone can take to negotiations is trustworthiness**. Remember that card-sharps in the Wild West had a short life-expectancy.

# Chapter 14
# Lobbying

*Bonjour, M. le Commission official. Un beau bureau, n'est-ce pas? And quelle lovely vase! Fragile? J'espère que rien mauvaise happens to it. Oh, j'ai le laisser tombée! Quelle butterfingers! Alors, cette Directive. J'ai les amis who don't like it. Non, pas de tout. Mais, si vous valuer votre Mercedes, il y a quelque changes sur cette position paper que vous might considerer? Excellent!*

*From* Lets's Parler Intimidation avec Le Commission

## Introduction

Anyone who has had the pleasure to be visited by sales people hawking dusters, double glazing or financial services will know what it is to be lobbied. First comes the mail-shot, the irritating phone call, or the more traditional foot in the door. Then you are assailed by the patter, the *10%-discount-seeing-as-it's-you* or *we'll-throw-in-this-set-of-kitchen-knives-absolutely-free-if-you-phone-now!* sales pitch. Worse even than this is the approach which undermines you with images of how shallow and unglamorous your life is. Hair loss. Draughty windows. Looming penury. Soon, people will laugh and point as you pass by in the street. Your children may suffer. Then comes the solution which will make your life whole again, be it a pension or new draught excluders.

Only the strong should read on, for all the ghastly skills of the salesperson – securing access, persuasive patter and anxiety-selling – must be at your command.

## Identifying the Target

Brussels has many players. How do you choose which ones to try to influence?

First, remember that negotiations have a shape and rhythm to them. They start in technical committees, progress through working groups, and only towards the end of the process do Ministers, Commissioners and parliamentarians take part. Further, the pantheon of Brussels deities will not wish to concern themselves too much with the minutiae of technical annexes or arcane drafting points. So even if you have the home phone number of the President's mother's cat, don't assume this is your best target.

Instead, concentrate on the players working on the dossier at the time, or likely to do so shortly. This means, in the early stages, the desk officers in the Commission, the officials from Member State administrations, and perhaps the researchers for interested MEPs. Later on, you may find that approaches to senior officials and politicians are needed to break a deadlock or win a difficult point. You should also consider those outside the negotiation who are likely to have an influence: journalists, pressure groups, trade associations and major companies.

You can track down your targets through the *Directory of European Institutions, Vacher's European Companion* and the like, or just phone up the relevant institutions and (after several tries and much passing between different departments) they should tell you: every organisation – even MI5 – has an official point for accepting enquiries.

## Access

But will they see you? For as you pass through this process, so do many hundreds of others. Cynics might say: 'If someone is powerful enough to be able to help you, they won't have time to see you.' This is the problem of **access**: that is, finding the combination of influence, contacts and initial approach that allows you the chance to set out your case. After all, why should a Commission official take time off from preparing for World Government to discuss bathing-water quality in Gothstanton or salmonella in drop scones? The main reasons are:

**They have to**
Most officials are expected to give a hearing to those from outside the organisation; middle and high-ranking officials, though, may pass you to those lower down, and any official might insist on you lobbying by letter. So, this reason on its own will not always be enough.

**They want to**
Many officials themselves wish to hear out all those with an interest because they see it as professional to do so. They may have some sympathy for particular interest groups, and may also want to know more. Never underestimate the potential for ignorance in others (especially about specific conditions in individual Member States). This shades into . . .

**They want something in return**
This really is the key: it is not realistic to expect busy people to give up time they could otherwise devote to their own work – and more importantly, to keep doing so for as long as it takes to complete your influencing strategy – unless you have something to offer in return. Usually, cash, fur coats and negotiable securities are not appropriate. Offering support, even building an alliance, is much more the thing; but the everyday currency of Brussels is **information**.

## Trading Information

In essence, if you know anything very much about a negotiation, you will probably know something that your interlocutor doesn't know. Even failing this, you are likely to go off to meet others, so there's always the chance of picking up fresh information which you can pass back next time you meet.

This willingness to trade information will open more doors than any other tactics, be they demands, pleas, or threats of painful retribution. So try to give the impression, when seeking a meeting, that you, your position, and what you might know about the positions of others are all highly interesting. Once you have access, keep in mind the need to trade information – and even better, to build an alliance – so that your access will continue.

## The Pitch

Once you are seated across the table from your target, business cards exchanged and comments about the dismal Brussels weather out of the way, you are faced with the dilemma of **the pitch**. In other words, how best to put over your case. There is, of course, no one *right* way, but there are points to consider:

- **Empathy** (What effect your case might have on your lobbying target?)
- **Going with the grain** (How can your case be presented to best fit their position?)
- **Changing perspectives** (How might you change their position, or perceptions, to advance your cause?)

*Empathy*
The first point to consider is the starting position of the person, or institution, you wish to influence. Even if the problem is being put to them for the first time, you should be able to predict possible reactions. The essence of lobbying is seeking to persuade someone to do something (or not do something). To persuade them, you need to understand what, in practice, they can and cannot do, so that you can concentrate on productive options.

For example, you might not like a new proposal to regulate cream teas sold to the public. So you might visit the Commission official charged with the task of preparing the legislation and say, 'We don't like the legislation.' But which is the more likely action the official would then take:

- To go to the Commissioner and say, 'Sorry, we'll have to scrap the draft Directive, the Nether Wallop Cream Tea Society are against it'?
- To note, file and forget your opposition?

Remember that the official's objective is to build an alliance around the emerging proposal: the more groups and interests it satisfies, the more likely it is to make progress. If you make it clear there are no changes that will satisfy you, then no changes will be made. You will get nothing.

Outright opposition only works when you have enough clout to dictate changes. If a majority of Member States tell the Commission that a proposal is unacceptable, the Commission will be forced to drop it; but this is rare. Usually, the Commission (or any other institution) will only start out on the path towards new legislation on the basis of a judgement that agreement is likely: that outright opposition will not be strong enough to block it. So if you are in outright opposition, you have two choices:

- Build an alliance strong enough to block it (and quickly).
- Play it smart, and drop or cover over your opposition to the principle, concentrating instead on opposition to the detail (and perhaps on securing improvements).

*Going with the Grain*
So what changes might a bureaucracy live with? In terms of legislation, these are three main areas which might be amended without compromising too far the basic objectives of the proposal:

- scope
- timing
- requirements

If legislation is unwelcome but unavoidable, you might make a case to have yourself, or your particular group, industry or sector, excluded from its scope. Or you could seek to modulate the timing: the provisions of the legislation could be phased in, giving time to adjust. Or you might press for the specific requirements to be modified: perhaps reports submitted every three years rather than annually, or standards relaxed or phased in. All would require modifications to the text of the proposal (and such changes, if significant in their **implications**, are still likely to be debated and possibly opposed). Nevertheless, all would allow the proposal to proceed.

In the face of such suggestions, the archetypal Commission official would then make a calculation: does the benefit of the modification (the removal of your opposition or even your added support) outweigh the cost (possible greater opposition from others, and a deviation from the original intention of the legislation)? This calculation will not always go in your favour, but at least there is a chance that it might.

---

**Anticipating the Response**

Lobbying is not a one-way street: you should prepare yourself for the more common reactions of those lobbied. You might think you are bowling well and piling on the pressure (cricketing metaphors courtesy of the Foreign Office), but they may then:

**Block** your case with a deadening response (*very interesting, will look into further, can't expect a response at this stage, will let you know how it goes*) so they can maintain the initiative (or decide to do nothing).

**Cut** the case away to someone else (*most interesting, love to help, but it's really more for DG III/the Commissioner/the ECJ/the Member State governments*) so that any further action will be for others.

**Glance** it away into space (*don't see the problem, perhaps you're worrying over nothing, should be fine once in place*) so that no one need take further action.

**Smash** the case back over your head (*no question of acting as you request, quite inappropriate even to ask me, thousands would die if your deranged proposal were enacted*). This response is rather rare and is likely to be an attempt to dispirit you, or as a defensive measure.

---

*Changing Perspectives: Motivational and Anxiety Lobbying*
The starting point, therefore, is the perspective of the individual or organisation you wish to influence. You have shown sympathy with their aims and tried to offer practical suggestions, even amendments. But this may not be enough. You may face hostility to your position if it still clashes with the aims of those being lobbied. Or, as is more common and

perhaps more awkward, those being lobbied *may just not care* about your problem.

One response to this is to seek to change the perspective of those being lobbied. They might be persuaded that there are benefits in moving towards your position, so that you create a positive **motivation**. More commonly, though, you will be showing that your problem is their problem too – creating an **anxiety**. If successful, you should be able to put forward possible ways of resolving the problem with a better chance of a favourable reception.

You might start by showing how the problem does not affect you alone: other Member States and other sectors may be affected, jobs and businesses lost, etc. The problem should also be brought closer to home. Suggest that, unless your difficulty can be resolved, there will be resistance to the whole Commission proposal: a tough ride in the Council, objections from the European Parliament, maybe even from other DGs or other Commissioners.

Then put forward solutions: ones which suit you, but are also practical. If the person being lobbied can see a way of delivering what you need without creating worse problems elsewhere, you are well on the way to convincing them that they should do so. Ideally, this final stage should be co-operative: you and the lobbyee working together to create and assess possible ways forward.

## Case Study: The Tea-pots Directive

How would this work in practice? Imagine that you are a manufacturer of novelty tea-pots, and the proposed Tea-pots Directive includes standards for spouts with which your latest product line, tea-pots in the shape of Canterbury Cathedral, would not comply. Of course, no one would ever actually make tea in your works of art, but rules are rules.

On the face of it, few Commission officials are likely to be bothered overmuch by the profitability of a single manufacturer when the safety of 350 million citizens is at stake and, just as importantly, when the Commissioner wants a draft Directive in three weeks.

But all is not lost. First, you make clear that you

appreciate the safety case and the pressure the Commission is under to produce safety standards, and explain your own difficulty. Then, you expand the size of the problem by showing that souvenir tea-pots across Europe – from the Tour Eiffel to the Parthenon, and including Brussels' own Mannequin Pis – could be affected. You hand over research commissioned by the European Ceramics Federation showing that thousands of jobs are at risk. You then pile on the pressure: the local MEP is worried, the unions are massing, and the German Chancellor is a noted collector of novelty china.

Now the official is suitably concerned. Instead of a minor technical problem she may face high-level political opposition. This will inevitably lead to delays. She sees endless meetings, stress, and the likelihood of a roasting from the Commissioner ahead of her. This is the time to mention possible solutions.

You might say that you don't want the Directive changed, but is there any need for it to cover novelty tea-pots? If no one uses them to make tea, there is no safety problem. Or you might say you don't want to block the Directive, but you do need more time to dispose of your stock: another year, perhaps. So perhaps the specifications should be left to a technical committee, which might take a year to finalise them. Or perhaps just some minor changes to the technical specification for spouts will solve your own problems.

Either way, the official sees the clouds part: the Commission would still be able to adopt the proposal formally, with a good chance of getting it adopted, and the public and the media could be reassured that everything is being done. A happy ending.*

## Lobbying the Institutions

*The Commission*
The Commission tends to be relatively open and approachable, with time pressure and overwork being the main

---

* If you *are* a manufacturer of novelty tea-pots, please note that the above approach is not guaranteed to work.

reasons for problems with access. Officials from national administrations naturally build up extensive contacts with officials in the Commission Services, and these can bring rewards on specific dossiers and to the Member State as a whole. The key is establishing trust through professional and personal contacts.

## Commission Cabinets

Government officials rarely have any dealings directly with cabinet members: this is usually done through the national Representations. Outside interests have a free hand to try to get access to cabinet members, but they are few in number and their in-trays are usually well stocked. Your initial pitch is likely to be by letter, rather than phoning up (trying 'Could I just drop by next week when I'm in Brussels?' is not recommended). See Chapter 15 for more on written approaches.

## The Council

The Council itself is best approached via the Member State government and administration. Remember that some countries – notably Germany and Spain – have constitutions which reserve powers for regional government, and lobbying there may be much more effective than with central government.

The Member States maintain Permanent Representations in Brussels, and these are usually open to all, though again time pressure will limit opportunities, and, in any case, formal responsibility for policy remains with officials and Ministers in capitals. Remember that other countries such as the United States also have Representations, and these can be useful allies.

The Council Secretariat is impartial and it would be most unusual for its officials to be lobbied. This said, there is no bar on civil servants establishing good working relations with Secretariat officials in the margins of working groups, so ensuring that the message is clearly understood (though the Permanent Representation would expect to be consulted before an official wrote to or raised any issue with the Secretariat).

*The European Parliament*

The Parliament has considerable powers to influence most Community legislation, and measures adopted under Article 189c of the Treaty – the co-decision procedure – may in effect be vetoed. The Parliament is also the most open of the Community institutions, with many of its meetings open to the public and most Members conscious that the Parliament depends on public support for much of its claim to a greater role in the Union. For these reasons, the Parliament has become a major target for lobbying.

The composition of the Parliament gives three avenues of approach to MEPs:

- on the basis of party policies
- on the basis of their support for particular interest groups or sectors
- on a national, regional or constituency basis

For all its openness, the Parliament has complex internal procedures and you need to be particularly careful about timing: not making your approach too late or too early, and showing you know how the EP functions and what options are open to those being lobbied.

---

**Hell's Lobbyists**

MEPs are always being lobbied: sometimes you need a little help to catch their attention.

In 1994 the Commission adopted a Directive (a single-market measure based on Article 100a, to be adopted by Qualified Majority Voting and co-decision with the Parliament) to limit the power of motorbikes. This, in effect, would have banned the largest and most powerful models such as Triumphs. Despite opposition from the UK (apart from Italy the only EU state where such bikes are manufactured), the Council reached a common position. Only the Parliament could block the measure, but why would they be interested in such a minority group?

But the biker lobby, alerted by the specialist press (*Performance Bike* running articles explaining the co-

decision procedure) and advised by the UK Representation, put together a first-class lobbying campaign. The
bikers lobbied to warn of the dangers to European
industry and the loss of liberty to peaceable (if leather-
clad and studded) citizens, and produced evidence to
show that larger bikes were less dangerous than smaller
ones (which, being cheaper, were bought by young
tearaways).

With the Parliament won over, the finale to this
campaign was a mass rally by thousands of bikers
outside the Industry Council meeting in Luxembourg
where the proposal was being debated: to the roar of
hundreds of motorbikes, eight Hell's Angels carried a
Triumph Bonneville in a coffin to be laid to rest on the
steps of the Council building.

The proposal was not adopted.

## The Etiquette of Lobbying

Finally, some tips on how lobbying meetings should be
conducted. As in any meeting, the mind has to juggle any
number of thoughts: about the subject, the handling of this
meeting, how late you may be for the next meeting, and did
you set the video to record *Inspector Morse*? You may find it
easier to have the messages on the etiquette of lobbying
boiled down into a few handy phrases:

- Make clear to those you are lobbying that you want to
  build a relationship which is on-going and two-way,
  particularly when it comes to information.
- Balance this by showing you know the need for tact and
  discretion.
- Always show you can see the issue from the perspective
  of those you are lobbying.
- Be polite and positive: seek to improve, not block, their
  work and aims.
- Match their mood: if they want to be brisk, or free-
  thinking, or to speculate on 'whither Europe?', or talk
  about which restaurants they prefer, go along with it.

- Have your main points on paper, ready to hand over, so they don't have to make notes (see Chapter 15).
- Start to leave as soon as they look bored or annoyed.

# Chapter 15
# Briefing

*Two figures, clad in overcoats, are feeding the ducks in St James's Park. George Smirkey, acting head of British Intelligence, is briefing his latest recruit, Gilbert.*

*'What do I need to know, sir? About this job?'*

*'We've heard from a source in Moscow Central,' said Smirkey, 'that the Circus may have a mole on the trapeze. The lamplighters have their eye on Esterhazy but our Friends think that our Cousins may have a line in to him. Or them. Or us. Anyway, M and Q agree with C and the PM's PS wants Five to lean on Auntie, shake the tree, see what falls. That could take us to Carla via Tinker. So I want you to babysit Control. Clear?'*

*'Could you just run over that last bit again, sir?'*

## Introduction

Briefing is the process of passing over information on a subject, either orally or on paper. A good brief should fill the gaps in the knowledge of the reader or hearer (the *user*), so that they end up knowing the story so far, the key facts, the positions of all other plays, the options and the recommended decision. It should also *not* include anything unnecessary, and should be so structured that the user can make the best of the information it contains.

Within this rough definition, each brief should have a purpose, based on the circumstances of the negotiation or decision you wish to influence. In drafting written briefing, you also need to bear in mind who the brief is for (your *customer* or customers); and with whom they will use the brief (the *final audience*). Oral briefing follows many of these same principles, but is much more straightforward.

## Considering your Customer

Briefing could be prepared for any number of 'customers':

- your boss, going to a meeting with an MEP
- a Minister negotiating in Council
- a Commission official, attending an internal Commission meeting
- a journalist, wanting background on a controversy
- yourself, at a working group

In each case, what they know, what they need to know, and how they would want the information set out should be readily apparent. For starters, there is the physical look of the brief:

- How large is it?
- How clear is the writing?
- Is there too much jargon and technical material?
- Have you spelt out any acronyms on their first appearance?
- What about the design (typeface and layout)?
- Is there a logic to the order of points and papers?
- Could you find what you were looking for in a hurry?

## The Contents of the Brief

Traditionally, written briefing for a meeting has the **objectives** up-front, so that the user can pick it up at the start of a meeting and know immediately why they are there and what they want from it. This might also include some guide as to possible fall-backs or secondary objectives. It should also have a clear **guide** or index to the structure of the briefing (unless it all fits neatly on a page or two) so that the user can move easily to the exact material they need. This would usually follow any previously agreed agenda for the meeting.

## The Elements of a Brief

Armed with these, the user can then move to individual points to make. Most users of briefing like these to be short and punchy (sometimes called bullet points):

- They can add their own wording themselves.
- Others prefer to have a full speaking note to read out.
- All a matter of taste.

On occasions, having the exact wording of, say, a statement to be read into the minutes of a Council meeting is clearly vital. The amount of background and supporting material is dependent on the nature of the subject and the type of meeting. As a minimum, though, any document which is to be referred to should be available in the briefing pack.

## Briefing at One Remove

Much briefing is prepared not for yourself or your superiors, nor even to inform and enchant possible allies or opponents, but for allies to use in *their* battles on your behalf. Here, the need for careful thought about the audience is critical. You may need to go through your briefing and strike out anything which:

- shows who prepared the briefing (this might mean specific references, such as 'The UK Government believes that . . .' or even removing your organisation's letterhead or logo)

- Relies heavily on arguments which the audience would not expect the user to deploy (it would be seen as odd, for example, for a Commission official responsible for environment protection to make too much of likely burdens on business)
- uses arguments which the audience will not be too impressed with (again, imagine the reaction of Commission officials to a line from one of their colleagues that a proposal offends against subsidiarity)

## Briefing for the Real Brussels

In looking at real briefing needs, there are three typical uses which correspond to the three main Community institutions: for the Parliament, the written briefing note; for the Commission, detailed background material on a proposal; and for the Council, briefing for Ministers attending the Council itself.

*Briefing the European Parliament*
Members of the European Parliament deal with dozens of pieces of legislation each year and so cannot be experts on every subject before them. Also, the Parliament has had a policy of openness to the public and to interest groups and some (mainly UK) MEPs represent specific constituencies. All this means that it is an excellent place to use briefing material to bolster your case.

The UK Government provides written briefing to UK MEPs on all Commission proposals. Traditionally, this briefing was based on the Explanatory Memorandum submitted to the UK Parliament, which describes the legislation and sets out the attitude of the UK Government, with particular emphasis on specific topics such as costs and subsidiarity. Experience showed that this was not the best approach: the two institutions do not have the same briefing needs and often have very different perspectives on Community legislation (and topics such as subsidiarity).

Effective briefing concentrates on:

- Specific problems with the proposal, including *why* it

poses problems for *specific* groups and individuals. For example, the proposal might be costly: better to make clear who will have to pay and why certain groups would suffer.
● Realistic solutions, based around textual amendments which would remove or ameliorate the problem. Outright opposition to the aims of the proposal may be appropriate, but is only likely when this matches the position of the EP as a whole (remember that the EP's veto in effect requires the political groups to co-operate).
● Points where EP support is likely, or at least conceivable, rather than points which matter to you. For example, saying that a proposal would require major changes to legislation in a Member State is not likely to be of concern to an MEP.
● The EP's own procedures, so that briefing is appropriate to the stage the proposal has reached within the Parliament. This is particularly important when briefing for the Parliament's second reading: only those amendments adopted at first reading will be considered, and briefing on anything else is usually a waste of effort which suggests ignorance and confusion on the part of those providing the briefing: not the right message to send!*

---

**Impartiality**
The principle is that UK officials should send or offer any briefing to all UK political groupings in the European Parliament. This rule is interpreted less absolutely when briefing rapporteurs, or with constituency matters, or when responding to direct requests for information. Also, attachés at the UK Representation tend to have closer working relationships with MEPs than home civil servants would with Westminster MPs. Nevertheless, party-political briefing is always left for Ministers and political advisers.

---

Both officials and others seeking to influence the Parliament may provide written briefing to any individual or group of

* Though there may be times when this self-imposed rule is waived by the Parliament. As in all things European, individual circumstances may override general rules.

MEPs (though to be impartial, UK officials do not offer briefing to one political group only: see box). This allows a brief to be tailored:

The **rapporteur** might be offered a full written briefing with an oral briefing as follow-up (though note the 'offered': it is always best to ask in advance what form of briefing they would like). Other **key players** (the chair and vice-chair of the committee and the leadership of the political groups) might well be offered the same.

MEPs with a **constituency interest** (such as a factory which would be affected by a proposal or particular social circumstances) would welcome specific warning on the implications as well as general background.

The **members of the committee** leading on the dossier might be sent a general paper setting out concerns and improvements (this need not be restricted to any national group). Again, the offer of a briefing meeting or presentation might be floated, but even if MEPs and their staff express interest, they may not turn up on the day (they are *very* busy).

**All MEPs**, or all national MEPs, might be sent a brief note on the main issues in the run-up to the plenary where the vote is to be taken, together with a **voting list**. The latter is most important: any brief short enough to fit on a single side of paper will not be detailed enough to make clear your position on each amendment (there may be hundreds). The voting list simply lists the amendment numbers marked FOR, AGAINST or ABSTAIN, so that those who agree with your position overall know how to vote for it in detail.

The best briefing is based on factual and impartial material presented clearly and succinctly. This is important for Member State administrations and others where MEPs might be suspicious that briefing is party-political.

*Briefing the Commission*
The same sorts of considerations apply as for the Parlia-

ment: briefing should be clear, honest, to the point, and sent to the right people at the right time. Nevertheless, there are differences of approach and interest which should be borne in mind:

● At the very start of the process, you might want to pass over very detailed background material – such as copies of current practice or domestic legislation, or specific evidence – to help influence the initial direction of a proposal.
● You may find allies in one part of the Commission or another who you can share material with, so helping their position. Again, this could be detailed and technical.
● Legal arguments often play better within the Commission, and also are particularly dear to the hearts of the Commission Legal Service (who can be very powerful allies indeed: the Commission is unlikely to act in direct disregard of an opinion from its own lawyers).

*Briefing the Council*
All items on or likely to be added to the Council agenda need some form of written briefing from the lead official. This brief serves three purposes:

(i) To explain the issues that need to be resolved and to provide a line to take for each.
(ii) To allow others within the Whitehall system a last chance to review the issues and comment on the proposed line.
(iii) To ensure that, should the lead official fall under the wheels of a bus on the way to Council, the show can go on.

Consequently, the brief must be **clear**, so that Ministers and others at Council can see the overall shape of the negotiations and understand what the key objectives are; but also **detailed**, so that others can understand the whole of the UK position in some detail before and, if necessary, at Council.

## The Structure of Council Briefs

The Presidency and the Council Secretariat produce a document some days before Council which summarises the outstanding issues which Ministers will need to resolve at

Council (see p. 166). The debate at Council will almost certainly follow the arrangement in this Secretariat Note (from Coreper to Council). Therefore, unless there is a good reason to the contrary, the brief for Council follows the pattern of the Secretariat Note as well.

Sometimes the Secretariat Note is not available in English until shortly before the Council. No matter. The French text may well be out much sooner; and the note to Council is likely to follow the same pattern as the note from the Secretariat to Coreper produced a week or two before.

## The Summary

However the brief is laid out, it should contain a summary of the overall position on the negotiation. Typically, this would say:

> The Nuts Directive is vital to the UK to ensure a proper supply of nuts in May.
>
> The two main remaining questions are: the **implementation date** (the UK, Germany and France want three years; all other Member States five) and the status of **mulberry trees** (Germany alone cannot accept the Presidency compromise).
>
> The secondary points (in Section II of the Secretariat Note) are not significant to the UK. MAFF (representing nut-gatherers) are content that the **walnut exemption** be extended until 2010 in return for compromise on the implementation date.
>
> We expect the Presidency to propose a compromise of: four years for the date; keeping the current text on mulberry trees; and asking all Member States to drop their reservations in Section II. **The UK could accept this compromise**.

Once this key information has been put over, the brief can go on to provide:

- the **speaking notes**
- the **background** to the proposal
- the latest estimates of the **costs and benefits** (including the impact on small and medium enterprises and any areas of uncertainty
- the **detail** on each remaining question
- any other potential **pitfalls**, with defensive material

Each element should, as far as possible, follow the pattern set by the Secretariat Note. In this way the user, whether Minister, Ambassador or official, can use the brief and the Note together to follow the debate. It also means that less important information (such as wording tabled by other Member States) which is in the Note need not be reproduced in the brief. The Note should be seen as part of the main brief, though a subordinate part.

If the brief is quite complicated, with a number of speaking notes or defensive lines to take, officials often include a short paragraph on the front page to explain how the brief is structured and where each element can be found quickly. It is best not to rely on flags, as a full Council brief (which may consist of twenty agenda items or more overall) will have quite enough flags already.

## Speaking Notes

The brief usually includes speaking notes for all interventions. It may also include one additional note which brings all the key points into a single speaking note, in case Ministers decide to make – or the Presidency to allow – only a single intervention. Make sure the brief makes clear which note is which!

All speaking notes should be crisp and to the point. Once drafted, try reading them out to colleagues: if they seem windy or clumsy, they need redrafting. Also, try to boil them down. A quick bit of sub-editing can produce interventions which are shorter and also have more impact:

*Before*:
The UK Government is of the opinion that further work is

needed on the proposal we are considering today to ensure that the measures relating to walnut production operations can be improved to make them acceptable to us.

*After*:
I believe that we need to keep working on this proposal to ensure that walnut farms are dealt with properly.

Many Member States listen to the UK in English rather than through the interpreters. When interventions are clear and forceful, this will come across directly and add to the impact of the material.

## Council Working Groups

The purpose of the briefing for Council working groups is similar to that for Councils, but the structure is usually quite different, for three reasons. First, the document on which it is based is, initially, the Commission's proposal and, subsequently, any revised text produced by the Commission or the Presidency/Council Secretariat. Second, the nature of the negotiations is different: initially there may be dozens of points of detail which the UK wishes to see changed, whereas for Council briefing these points have either been resolved or whittled down to a few remaining significant issues. Third, the target audience for the brief is not only the negotiating team but also all those following the negotiations across Whitehall, notably EUD(I) at the FCO; the Cabinet Office; and other interested departments.

Therefore, for Council working groups, the brief should consist of:

- a short resumé of the objective (particularly if the subject is new)
- a guide to the key negotiating points, with some sense of the priorities
- the UK position point-by-point, including alternative wording to modify the text wherever possible

Speaking notes are not needed (attachés and officials are paid to write their own scripts), except on very rare occasions where the exact wording of an intervention matters.

The main customers of these briefs are the attachés at UKRep, and it makes sense to discuss with them the exact format you use before starting to draft. If they are happy with a slimmed-down version, as is often the case, this saves work all round. The brief should be circulated in advance wherever possible and should reach UKRep by the day before the meeting at the latest. Usually, the attaché will be available to discuss the brief and tactics for the meeting in the morning before the working group starts (but check beforehand).

During fast-moving negotiations, where a dossier can be scheduled for discussion in the working group almost every week, producing a full brief may not be possible. Again, colleagues will usually understand (point out the facts of life if not), and a note of the key points should be sufficient.

## Oral Briefing

In addition to the written material, officials may be called on to provide oral briefing to Ministers before and at a Council. This happens:

(i) at the briefing meeting with the Minister, UKRep and lead officials in the week before Council
(ii) at the meeting on the morning of Council with the Minister (if available); UKRep (usually the Ambassador or deputy) and attachés, and the press attaché if available); and officials from other departments
(iii) at other *ad hoc* meetings during the Council
(iv) in the Council chamber during the debate.

Oral briefing requires different skills, but the aim remains the same: to pass on the information needed **and no more**. Thinking through what the listener needs to know is still the key: one advantage is that the recipient of the briefing is before you: giveaway clues to having drifted off the subject include yawns, glazed eyes and frequent shifts of posture.

## Pre-Council Oral Briefing

Summarise the essential problem or key objective straight away: avoid telling 'the story so far' in too much detail and try to link the proposal to concrete examples or likely effects in the real world. If a proposal would ban a particular chemical, don't just name it but explain what it does and who would be affected.

As with written briefing, Ministers in particular will want to know the answers to the same underlying questions which anyone coming upon a subject would pose:

- What is this all about?
- Why does it matter?
- What will it cost?
- What do others think?
- Who'll back me up?

For any proposal, a few sentences should be enough to cover all these points, allowing time for more detailed discussion on specific points or on questions of policy or tactics. You might even write yourself a short speaking note to make sure the essence is covered in your first comments.

> Poly-Globulated Bi-Cyclotron is an insecticide used by many European nut-gatherers, but recent evidence suggests it can be extremely harmful to squirrels. The Commission, lobbied by SOS (Save Our Squirrels) and others, have proposed phase-out by 2005. The UK has already announced a ban from 2002, even though MAFF estimates the switch to other chemicals will raise costs by 3% for the average UK nut-gatherer. UK domestic opinion is strongly in favour of the ban.
>
> Our first objective is a phase-out by, but not before, 2002: we are strongly supported by France, Ireland, Germany and Sweden but opposed by Denmark. Our other main objective is to prevent a compromise with a phase-out date later than 2005.

Remember that some terms can be anything but clear: for

example, if it is proposed to alter the standard for spore emissions from mushroom factories from 1,000 spores per hour to 500 sph, this is a *higher* standard (in the sense of a 'better' or 'tougher' standard) but also a *lower* standard (in the sense that the new standard is a lower figure than the old standard). Much time can be wasted and confusion caused in discussions if the terms are not made clear at the start.

*Briefing in the Council Chamber*
The Minister is flanked by the lead official and the Permanent or Deputy Permanent Representative. Broadly, the former is there to offer policy advice, while tactical and procedural guidance is supplied by the latter. Those who have not experienced this responsibility can find it intimidating in the extreme: decisions with huge administrative and cost implications can be taken in minutes and the negotiations are often fast-moving and difficult to follow. You will be trying to follow the debate, work out the implications, draft modified lines to take and answer questions from the Minister all at the same time. All this with no safety-net.

Worse, you have to remain calm. This is not just for your own sake but to reassure those around you. Your role is to provide clear and measured advice, and those who have to take decisions on the basis of that advice need to feel it is well-judged and authoritative. If you appear rattled, they will have less confidence and may be less effective as a result.

On the plus side, all the other delegations are going through the same turmoil.

## Briefing the Media

The classic media brief, the press notice or press release, is rarely the best way to influence media coverage of European decision-making: it lacks sufficient depth, is not properly targeted, and can be rather unsubtle. If you want a 'Europe Bans British Cream Tea' story, fine: but raising the stakes in this way may well prove counter-productive.

Therefore, most media briefing is oral, with the offer of

supporting documents or an *aide-memoire* to back up the message. Oral briefing is also more flexible in fast-moving negotiations, and often more discreet. The discussion of lobbying in Chapter 14 applies here: once again, see it from the journalists' point of view. Do they want material on which to base informed comment, or just a good story? What angle might you have which will be of interest to them, their editor and their readership? What can you offer in return for coverage of your concerns?

## The Brussels Press Corps

There is a large press corps based in Brussels: some cover the 'big' stories for the national newspapers and main broadcast media. The BBC and ITN have Brussels offices. In addition, there are any number of specialist journalists who look for relevant stories and general background on trends in attitudes and forthcoming decisions, and who can cope with more technical material. Reuters and other information suppliers span the spectrum from headline news to detailed market intelligence for subscribers. There are also independent journalists (known as 'stringers') who prepare and sell stories on to the media.

UK Government media relations at the Brussels end are handled by the UK Representation. The press attaché and colleagues know most of the journalists and so are well placed to give briefing *off the record* (non-attributable background) to put the UK case over on controversial issues or even to place positive stories. Before each Council the relevant attachés hold a press briefing and also brief on its progress and outcome.

## Defensive Briefing

Keeping the media briefed is not all about taking the initiative: just as important to successful influencing is reacting to stories generated elsewhere or potential press interest in news stories arising from your own actions or announcements. The key is making sure you have an answer (a 'line to take') for the questions you can foresee. In a large organisation, such as a government department, preparing and distributing such briefing is a key part of the task of the press office. All potential outlets need the briefing: officials and delegations, UKRep, other posts in European capitals.

Policy officials, in turn, keep their press office in touch with developments by copying them relevant papers, and particularly background papers which summarise the key points. They produce in advance a line for all events with potential press interest, such as policy announcements.

## Tips on Briefing

Briefing is, in part, a matter of providing the ammunition for your team. This means that a good brief has to provide not only your position, priorities and background information, but also the raw material for the negotiating gambits discussed in Chapter 13.

This is a chance to let your imagination off the leash. Interventions explaining problems and suggesting compromises, even circulating texts, can only get you so far. You need sales skills, perhaps even a touch of the fairground quack or confidence trickster. Even something as simple as a visual aid can have a real impact (see box). Points which appear complex in words can be explained much more clearly (and memorably) in a diagram or flow-chart.

---

**The Factory**
The Commission table their proposal on major accident hazards in factories to the Environment Working Group. With it comes a photograph of a factory for each delegation, to help explain certain provisions. The Commission team then begin to explain the proposal, only to find that no one is listening: all the attachés are staring transfixed at the photograph. 'So that's what they look like,' they say to each other in nine languages. 'They've got chimneys and everything.' The horror of the scene is not lost on the officials from capitals: the attachés, poised to draft yet another piece

of legislation on factories, seem never to have seen one before.

Particular points can be emphasised with props. During a Council discussion on extending the controls on marketing chemicals, one Minister produced some bleach and disinfectant containers (raided by a resourceful official from the Council cleaners) to show his colleagues the sort of everyday product they were dealing with. The controls were dropped. Anything which fixes a point more firmly in the minds of other delegations should be considered (see box).

---

**Whisky Galore**

The same proposal on major accident hazards in factories risked bringing dozens of whisky warehouses into the control system. The UK had a scientific case: in a fire, whisky barrels (being made of wood) burn rather than explode and so are not a major hazard. But such cases are often hard to put over, so another case – a case of Scotch whisky – was produced to back it up. When the point was raised in Council, each Minister was presented with a miniature bottle of House of Commons whisky. The UK point was taken, no doubt solely on its merits.

---

There is plenty of scope for more mundane material. Where you already have experience of an approach or practice, deploying examples of successes might help to reassure others that the proposal under discussion is workable. Also, the positions of outside interests might be included, particularly those operating Community-wide. The positions of other Member States is basic but valuable material. It allows negotiators to look for allies and spot possible opponents and (as far as possible) tailor their interventions to win over as many as possible.

## Taking the Gloves Off

Finally, a slightly hazardous thought: occasionally, an organisation, institution or Member State will take a seemingly principled stand on an issue, but may have a poor record itself, perhaps not complying with international agreements, or may not even be affected at all by the proposal. This may be worth recording in the brief, though with some guide as to the reaction and sensitivity so that the user of the brief can judge whether and how to deploy it. Ideally, and in practice most of the time, debate in the Union is courteous and reasonable, but occasionally the brickbats fly, and it is always comforting to have one or two to hand to throw back. For one thing, it makes others less likely to go in for public posturing and unfair criticism if they know you are prepared to hit back.

# Chapter 16
# Logistics

*It is dusk. Two men are standing beside an aeroplane ready for takeoff.*

BIFFO:  So, Buffy, this is it.
BUFFY:  Yes, Biffo. The Big One.
BIFFO:  I say, I . . . I wish I was going too.
BUFFY:  Yes, old chap. But this is a job I can do better alone.
BIFFO:  Yes, yes, I see that. Well, pip-pip.
BUFFY:  Good show. Piece of cake, old man.

*They salute, then Buffy climbs aboard the British Midland shuttle to a crescendo of stirring patriotic music. The engines roar, the plane moves off, turns, then lumbers up into the gathering dark: Destination Brussels.*

## Introduction

Time spent preparing your position will be wasted if you can't get into the meeting room on the day; and however well you are prepared on paper you won't perform at your best if you've slept in a cardboard box the night before because you hadn't made a hotel reservation.

But more than this, knowing as much as possible about the logistics of trips to meetings removes one major source of anxiety. Travelling is stressful at the best of times (let alone on the Northern Line), so this chapter provides suggestions on preparing for travel, getting there and getting about, places to stay, and places to go when the meetings are over.

> Brussels has two official languages, French and Flemish. English is widely understood, and in some of the Flemish-speaking areas outside the centre may be better received than French: the linguistic divide is sensitive. Place-names are usually repeated in both languages on signs: in this chapter, French or Flemish names are used without any rational pattern at all.

## Formal Meetings

Those attending formal EU meetings should take certain documents:

- passport
- Form E111 (health insurance: application forms available from post offices)
- foreign currency (bureaux de change are not always open late)
- a copy of the telegram or fax calling the meeting (for the security desk)

UK officials should also take the details of Her Majesty's bank account, so that travel expenses may be refunded directly by the Council and Commission.

Meetings are held at several buildings in Brussels, with the bulk of Council and working group meetings in the Justus Lipsius, and Commission-chaired committees and expert groups in the Borschette. Most meetings are held in the EU Quarter in Brussels, for which the nearest métro station is Schuman:

JUSTUS LIPSIUS building: rue de la Loi 185 (Council)
Albert BORSCHETTE conference centre: rue Froissart (Commission)
BREYDEL: avenue d'Auderghem (Commission HQ)
CORTENBURG 1: avenue de Cortenburg 1 (Commission)
EUROPEAN PARLIAMENT: rue Belliard 97 (métro: Troon or Maelbeek)
BERLAYMONT: rue de la Loi 200 (Commission: currently being refurbished)

Meetings are also held from time to time at the Economic and Social Committee building, rue Ravenstein 2 (métro: Gare Centrale) and the Palais d'Egmont on the place du petit Sablon (métro: Porte de Namur)

Visitors need to obtain a pass to gain access to buildings and meetings, and should **allow plenty of time** as the security desks can be very busy in the twenty minutes or so before meetings start, particularly in the Council buildings. You usually need only show a copy of the telegram calling the meeting, but you should take your passport as well: the guards at the Parliament building in Strasbourg, for example, may not be used to visiting officials from Member States. If you are required to hand in your passport, **remember to collect it afterwards!**

Officials visiting Brussels frequently may be entitled to a permanent photopass: the Permanent Representations can provide a 'letter of attestation' to present to the Council security desk in the Justus Lipsius building. This pass should allow access to all Council, Commission and Parliament buildings (though check when you collect it!).

Most meetings start at 10 a.m. and end at 6 p.m., with a lunch break from 1 p.m. to 3 p.m., but these times can vary, so **check the telegram** and listen carefully for announcements from the chair during the meeting. Meetings often overrun, and if this is likely and your attendance is vital throughout the meeting, make sure you have flexible travel arrangements and a hotel reservation. If you cannot stay for the whole meeting, make arrangements in advance for someone to cover for you: don't assume that attachés from the Permanent Representation can do this.

## Hotels

You should make your hotel bookings before you leave: the main hotels in the EU Quarter in Brussels can be booked up well in advance, particularly during major Council meetings. The following hotels are used by officials (though none are specifically recommended and this guide accepts no responsibility if you end up sharing your room with roach-like wildlife):

|  | Tel. | Fax. |
|---|---|---|
| Europa Hotel, 107 rue de la Loi (used for Councils) | 230 1333 | 230 3682 |
| Hotel Archimède, 22 rue Archimède | 231 0909 | |
| City Garden, 59 rue Joseph II | 230 0945 | 230 6437 |
| Pullman Astoria, 103 rue Royale (used by Ministers) | 217 6290 | 217 1150 |
| Charlemagne, 25/27 blvd Charlemagne | 230 2135 | 230 2510 |
| Scandic Crown, 250 rue Royale | 220 6611 | |
| Queen Anne, blvd E Jacqmain 110 (English-style breakfast) | 217 1600 | 217 1838 |
| Metropole, 31 place de Brouckère (amazing toilets) | 217 2300 | |
| Marie-Jose, 75 rue de Commerce (supposed to be cheap) | 217 1890 | |
| La Legende, rue du Lombarde (slightly scruffy) | 512 8290 | |
| Sabina, rue du Nord (cheap) | 218 2637 | |

## Currency

Belgium and Luxembourg have a currency union, and Belgian francs (BF or BEF) and Luxembourg francs (FLux) should be accepted in both countries at 1:1. Cash can be obtained from banks or from UK bank accounts (if you have an internationally valid card) through thousands of cash machines. These are marked 'Mr Cash' or 'BanContact' and all cards should work in all machines. Belgian cash machines, however, often give out only the large-denomination 2,000-franc notes which many shops and taxis make a huge fuss about accepting.

Eurocheques, when backed by a Eurocheque card, are accepted almost everywhere. Visa and Access/Mastercard are usually taken, but do check first!

## Getting to Brussels

Brussels is served by frequent Eurostar trains from Waterloo and Ashford to Gare du Midi; and flights from Heathrow (British Airways, British Midland, Sabena), Gatwick (BA), Stansted (Air UK) and London City (Sabena) to Brussels Zaventem. Most regional airports have less frequent air services to Brussels and more cities now have through trains to the continent.

---

**Expect the Unexpected . . .**
The BM shuttle to Brussels always leaves from Gate 34 at Heathrow. Or almost always. One of our Brussels-based officials, overly familiar with the route, wandered through Terminal 1 thinking of nothing but UK water policy. Boarding the plane, he was surprised to be addressed by a South African Airways stewardess. Surprised, that is, until he found he had boarded the evening flight to Johannesburg. Visions of replacing the morrow's Coreper meeting with a pleasant free trip to the sun were dashed, though, by the thought that the wrath of an Ambassador is no less fearsome when 6,000 miles away.

---

# Getting About in Brussels

Brussels has an excellent and cheap public transport system operated by STIB/MIVB. Trains (the Airport-City Express) run every twenty minutes from the airport via Gare du Nord to the dismal Gare Centrale (journey time fifteen and twenty minutes). Go to Gare Centrale to connect with the métro, but get off at Gare du Nord for a taxi (same price and speed to the EU Quarter from both). A taxi trip to or from the airport should take twenty minutes but the route can be heavily congested in the evenings.

---

**Satan's Taxis**

Brussels taxis are very expensive. You should also be prepared to be passed a well-thumbed street atlas and asked to navigate: the drivers often haven't a clue where they are or where you want to go, unless it's the airport. But beware: this trip costs the equivalent of £20 or more (though you, as a highly trained negotiator, may be able to do a deal). This, apparently, is because taxis registered in Brussels cannot pick up fares at the airport (in the neighbouring commune of Zaventem), and vice versa, so they have to return empty. Beware, too, of taxi touts at the airport: their taxis may well not be insured, and personal injury is an ever-present danger on Belgium's roads.

One positive tip: the taxi driver may offer you a deal where you pay for a return trip at a discount: you get a ticket you can use with any taxi of the same group when you want to return to the airport. Oddly, this *isn't* a scam and really can save you money.

---

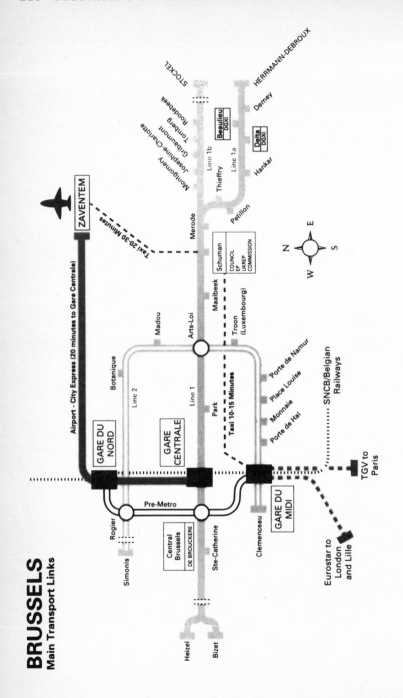

BRUSSELS
Main Transport Links

Tickets for travel on the métro, tram and bus network should be bought either at métro stations (the sign is a white 'M' on a blue background) or as you board the bus or tram. They last for one hour. Day and weekly passes and *carnets* (a good-value ticket which allows for ten trips) are also available from métro stations. Note that the métro does not run very frequently: usually every ten minutes, and only every twenty minutes in the evening.

Tickets should be stamped each time you get on a métro, tram or bus, even within the hour of travel each ticket allows: the machines are bright orange and will automatically know whether to cancel another part of the ticket or not. There are fines for fare-dodging: worse would be the embarrassment arising from dozens of elderly Belgians looking on disapprovingly.

Each route has a number and the direction is designated by the terminus: to travel on the métro from Gare Centrale to Schuman you would take the *Métro ligne 1*, *direction Herman-Debroux* or *Stokkel*. The return trip would be on the same line towards *Heysel* or *Bizet*. For Gare Midi and the Eurostar, the route to Schuman is on *ligne 2* towards *Simonis*, then change at *Arts-Loi* on *ligne 1*, returning on *ligne 2* towards *Clemenceau*. The same applies to trams and buses. Note that many stations have two names, French and Flemish.

## Eating, Drinking and Being Merry

All the main Commission and Council buildings have canteens serving reasonably good hot and cold food usually from 12.30 to 14.00 (exact times vary): the prices are quite fair by Brussels standards and so there can be long queues. They all have coffee bars too, which also usually sell sandwiches and cakes.

Outside, the European district in Brussels is equipped with any number of unimpressive bars and restaurants: the few really good ones soon fill up or are quite expensive compared to the UK (or both). You can get a goodish pizza, pasta or *steak frites* at any of the Italian jobs around the Berlaymont: the sandwich shops around Schuman are in general quite poor: Brussels eagerly awaits its first branch of Pret à Manger.

These restaurants are often used for formal entertaining:

L'Atelier, rue Franklin (expensive but popular; rare abundance of vegetables)
Perry's Grill, rue Froissart (good, though it looks like a Berni Inn)

Chez Carlo, rue Charlemagne (good food with a personal touch)

Le Vimar, place Jourdan (stuffy, but excellent fish, and convenient for the EP)

Le Stevin, rue St Quentin (**not** rue Stevin!; reliable, garden open in summer)

Brussels also has a few Parisian-style brasseries: Falstaff's (by the Bourse) serves good formula food quickly and with élan and is a favourite of at least one Chancellor of the Exchequer; Au Charlot's (opposite the Borschette), though smaller, does the same thing (but avoid Fridays, when the UKRep *bon viveurs* move in).

In the evening, the centre of Brussels has dozens of restaurants to tempt visitors, particularly around the Grand-Place and Ste Catherine: the best of these (Chez Vincent, Chez Jean, Le Volle Gas) are very good and most are more than adequate. Belgian specialities include *moules* (mussels) in season; *waterzoie* (soup with a large piece of fish or chicken and vegetables in it); *carbonade flammande* (braised flamingo in beer sauce); and *stoemp* (mashed potatoes mixed with a vegetable of choice, such as carrots or cabbage, and served with sausages: apparently, it closely resembles the Scots dish rumbledythumps).

Belgium used to own a large chunk of Africa, and in some districts this influence is reflected by delicacies such as ostrich and crocodile on menus and in supermarkets. Salads, sadly, are usually rubbish: typically, limp lettuce, boiled potato, tinned sweetcorn and green beans, sitting in milk.

*Chocolates*
Those fortunate enough to travel to Brussels often pay a 'chocolate tax' to their colleagues back home. For the sake of your bank balance, try to buy them in town rather than at the airport. The Neuhaus and Leonidas chains are both good.

*Beers*
They're all marvellous (though the fruit beers, which taste of Ribena, are an acquired taste), but use caution. The weakest

draft beers (Jupiler, Maes, Stella Artois) are much more alcoholic than in the UK, while the strength of others is reflected in their names: Judas; Mort Subite; Duvel (devil); Delirium Tremens. Best to sample them the evening **after** the meeting.

## Other Entertainments

Most meetings in Brussels and Luxembourg are too short to make boredom a problem (except in the meetings themselves), but if you need other distractions, Brussels in particular has several excellent cinemas, showing many films in English (those marked 'VO'): the Acropole (métro: Porte de Namur), the UGC City 2 (Métro: Rogier) and the UGC De Brouckère (métro: de Brouckère). There are also theatres, museums, art galleries (lots of Magrittes), concert halls and even a museum of water and sewage: almost everything to do is to be found in the English-language *Bulletin* (out each Friday) and in the daily and evening papers such as *Le Soir*. If you are stuck in Brussels over a weekend, Antwerp (a lively port city), Bruges (famous for lace-making) and Liège are about an hour away by train; Aachen and Maastricht are two hours away, and all are worth a visit.

For occasional visitors, sports facilities are effectively limited to those provided in hotels. In Brussels, the Sheraton has a swimming pool; in Luxembourg, about the only good thing about the Sofitel is that it too has a pool. There are a small number of municipal pools, the easiest to get to being Poseidon (métro: Tomberg). Rather oddly, the Belgian authorities frequently forbid bathing in swimming shorts (briefs only) or without a bathing hat.

## Shopping

Brussels prices are high compared to the UK. The main shopping centres are the rue Neuve, including the City 2 complex (métro: Rogier); the fabled Woluwe shopping centre (métro: Roodebeek); and the city centre (métro: Gare Centrale or de Brouckere).

## Local Information

- You should carry your passport – or a photocopy – about with you: the police have the right to ask for identification.
- Tips are included in the price in restaurants and taxis, but not in cinemas and public or bar toilets, where something around 10BF would be expected.
- By law you should take the VAT (TVA in French) receipt with you when you leave a restaurant.
- British newspapers are available from kiosks in the main Council and Commission buildings, from most other newsagents, and from W.H. Smith (blvd. Adolphe Max 71). At weekends, the Librarie de Rome on Avenue Louise is the best bet. In Luxembourg, try the kiosk at the railway station.

## Medicine

Medical treatment is Belgium is very good but is provided through compulsory private insurance companies (*mutualités*), so **carry form E111** with you. In any case, you may have to pay and then claim the money back from the Benefits Agency (so keep your receipts). UKRep or the British Embassy have a list of English-speaking doctors and dentists. **In an emergency, phone 100 for an ambulance**.

There are any number of pharmacies around Brussels selling analgesics (paracetamol, aspirin and ibuprofen are spelt the same in French, though pronounced differently) and antacids (Maaldrox is widely available). Lemsips are available under the brand name *Lem-grip*. Medicines are not cheap: that, and the national attachment to hypochondria, accounts for the fact that pharmacies look so prosperous. If you are intent on falling ill, try to do so in the Parliament building, as there is a doctor on the premises.

> **Only in Brussels**
> One UK official was struck down by illness during a meeting. An ambulance came and within minutes he

was speeding to hospital down the rue de la Loi. But this is Belgium, and the ambulance soon crashed into another vehicle. From the floor of the ambulance, covered in displaced bandages, swabs and oxygen cylinders, our man could just hear the ambulance team arguing with the other driver. As the argument turned to blows, he drifted into unconsciousness (often the best state to be in when dealing with Belgian traffic).

## Driving in Brussels

Don't. Belgians themselves admit they have the casual, devil-may-care approach to driving of the French or Italians, but without any of the skill. The recently introduced driving test hasn't helped, and driving is consequently a nightmare. The cavalier attitude extends to zebra crossings: don't expect the traffic to stop.

## Crime

Brussels is a relatively safe city, but don't relax completely: at night, be particularly careful around métro stations, the stations at Gare du Nord and Gare du Midi, and when using cashpoints (more than one official has been attacked). If threatened, the standard advice is to hand over the money: the 'have-a-go-hero' approach is not recommended. **In an emergency, phone 101 for the police**.

The police are occasionally unpleasant to those reporting petty thefts, even where this is necessary for insurance purposes, but if one police station is unhelpful, try another: each Brussels commune (there are nineteen) has its own police force, so you can shop around.

If documents go astray, or for other cases of lost property, try the following numbers:

| | | |
|---|---|---|
| **Airport:** | 723 6011 | (47918 in Luxembourg) |
| **STIB:** | 515 2394 | (47961 in Luxembourg) |
| **Train:** | 219 2640 | (49901 in Luxembourg) |

**Elsewhere:**           nearest police station

**For the emergency fire service, phone 100**. For the coast-guard, anti-poison centre, AIDS advice line (SIDA in French) and the rest, consult the phone book.


## Settling Down

Many people come to work in Brussels, on *stages* or other secondments for one of the institutions, as lobbyists, lawyers, or for one of the many international companies who have set up there. Most stay a few months, perhaps two or three years, while others settle. Brussels has leafy suburbs, schools, clubs and other facilities to cater for this semi-expatriate, multinational community. Finding accommodation is relatively straightforward and the price is not great by the standards of other capital cities, and once the nightmare brush with Belgian bureaucracy needed to register with your commune (local authority) is over, it does offer an excellent quality of life.

The impact of the European institutions on Brussels has been colossal, with economic benefits balanced by soaring prices and unsympathetic redevelopment. A large proportion of Brussels' population is non-native, including many thousands from outside Belgium. Though many incomers comment on how difficult it is to meet 'real' Bruxellois, the tolerance shown towards these newcomers is very impressive.


## Luxembourg

British Airways and Luxair both fly daily to Luxembourg (the airport, rather improbably, is called Findel). Flights and trains from Brussels to Luxembourg are more frequent: the train takes about two hours: some services depart from the stations at Schuman and Gare Leopold as well as the main central stations.

There isn't that much of Luxembourg (either the city or the country) to get about in. The main hotels run courtesy buses to and from the airport. There are buses from the airport to the centre and from the centre and railway station to the Kirchburg, the bizarre European district resembling a science park where the Council building, DG V of the Commission and the European Court of Justice are all located. If you do not have time for this leisurely route, take a taxi from the airport (allow about twenty to thirty minutes in case of heavy traffic).

Luxembourg has three hotels which are used frequently by visiting officials. The Sofitel (the former Pullman) is the only one near to the Council building on the Plateau de Kirchburg (the European centre) and is as a consequence profoundly overpriced, though the standard has recently improved. The Grunewald, nearer the centre of Luxembourg, has character and a good restaurant, while the Hotel Intercontinental is good, if a little bland. Both these are approximately a fifteen-minute taxi ride from the Kirchburg.

Restaurants tend to close early and many don't open at all on Sundays and Mondays. The style of cooking is heavily influenced by neighbouring Germany, and, as in Belgium, beer is drunk at least as much as wine. The central square has some pleasant restaurants, and with luck there may be a brass band playing as well.

It's difficult to imagine in Luxembourg, but in an emergency **phone 012 for all services**.

# Chapter 17
# At Council

*John Green had recently taken over negotiations on methane emissions from zoos for the Department of the Environment (his predecessor having to move on after developing an allergy to elephants). The Zoo Emissions Directive was due for agreement at the next Environment Council so John was in at the deep end. He has kindly agreed to allow his diary entries for the crucial days to be reprinted.*

**31 March**
I fly out to Brussels. Manage to grab a lift to the hotel with Phil Ditchins, who's borrowed the ministerial limo. Meet up with my oppos from the other Member States in the bar. Swap a few yarns and rumours. Early night.

**1 April**
**8 a.m.** Breakfast with the rest of the team, then head towards the Council building for the pre-meeting round-up. But the road in front of the Council building is filled with Belgian riot police cowering behind razor-wire barricades as hundreds of old ladies beat them over the head with brollies. Apparently it's a protest about some measure before the Consumer Affairs Council, which is also meeting today, arranged by a group of MEPs. Then comes a barrage of missiles. One lands near me: it seems to be a scone topped with clotted cream, but of course that's not possible.

A friendly copper directs me round to the side entrance and I work my way through the maze of gleaming corridors to the UK delegation rooms. It's full of UKRep and DOE people running around trying to get things copied or faxed back to London. I feel a bit of a spare part. At 9 a.m. sharp, Mr Bashem, the Deputy Permanent Representative, sweeps in for the briefing meeting.

He starts with the Electrical Exposure Directive and he isn't happy. Apparently the speaking note is far too long and the brief doesn't follow the format of the Council document. The officials are thrown out on their ears to rewrite the whole thing. I'm glad I read the minute through which commissioned the briefing, but it's still uncomfortable when he turns to me.

'Have you cleared this with MAFF?'

Phew. No problem there, so I nod.

'And what about Article 9? This stuff about fines for unauthorised emissions of crocodile urine. Are Home Office lawyers happy?'

My mind fills with blind terror. I checked with the Home Office, of course. But did *they* check with their lawyers?

'Errrrrrrrrrrrrrrrrr. Not sure.'

'Well, you'd better find out, laddie. Right, bathing water quality.'

The spotlight turns to Malcolm Bleat, so I can escape. I'd checked with Peter Wagers from UKRep that I'd not be on until at least 11 a.m. (10 a.m. London), so I've time to kill. The waiting around starts.

At about 10.30 the DPR, UKRep and the shell-shocked radiation people clear off to the Council chamber, ready for the '10 a.m. start'. A quiet descends. The UKRep secretary is knitting, the Press Officer is reading the morning papers.

And the quiet goes on. And on. I check with Home Office and all is fine. Still nothing happening. The officials with items further down the agenda, able to fly over during the morning, trickle in. The TV monitor which displays the agenda shows there's no progress yet. I wander into the next office, where the officials over for the Consumers Council are waiting around. I spot Ron Noakes: we were on a course at the Civil Service College together.

'What are you over for?'

'Tea-pots Directive. An orientation debate.'

Ron is looking unusually dapper. Gone is the gravy-stained M & S suit in grey with twin vents. Instead, he's wearing a snazzy Italian suit in bright-green shot silk. He spots my amazed expression and looks embarrassed.

'Er, well, I've had so many meetings with Commission officials and colleagues in other Member States, putting together this deal on tea-pots, I got sick of looking scruffy. But I haven't gone native.'

'You could've fooled me. I bet you'll be holidaying abroad from now on.'

'Well, I though we might take the caravan to St Tropez this summer . . .'

I drift down to the coffee bar, have a chat with the French and the Germans. They are as bored as me. We wonder what the Finns may have up their sleeves on camels. And whether the deal to buy off the Greeks will stick (this is to reclassify sloths and wombats as 'vegetables' on the basis that they fail to meet the Annex IV animal speed criteria). Then back to the delegation room.

**1 p.m.** Various ashen-faced radiation people flit in and out, trying to clear a compromise text with the Treasury. Then the Minister arrives in a flurry of bags, coats and officials. He gives a cheery wave and is straight into the Council chamber.

**2 p.m.** I suddenly feel hungry and head up to the bar for a sandwich. The bloke behind the bar tells me they'll have some more in an hour.

'M'sieur 'as just bought ze last one,' he says, pointing along the bar. It's Phil Ditchins, who smirks before tucking into the remainder of his baguette. I should've remembered the golden rule of Councils: *eat often, drink slowly*.

**2.15 p.m.** Back in the delegation room. The UKRep press attaché has heard the Council is deadlocked because the Germans can't accept the radiation proposal unless one of the annexes is completely rewritten. There'll be a parallel working group and my item's on straight after lunch.

**3.20 p.m.** The Minister and the rest of the delegation return from the formal lunch. There's a quick exchange, reporting back on what's been discussed, planning the afternoon's session, then they're back to the Council. We're due on again at four.

**5 p.m.** This is it. Peter Wagers sweeps me along corridors and up into the Council chamber. It's decked out in wooden panelling with gloomy lighting. We fight through the scrum to the UK seats and I sit next to the Minister.

'All OK on this?'

'Yes, Minister. The Finns may cause a problem on camels, but the Presidency has a compromise text in reserve which we can live with. And its cleared with MAFF.'

'Good. Let me know when it gets interesting.'

The Minister turns to the Ambassador to discuss some project for a jam factory in Poland. The Minister's been lobbied about it and wants to know what it's all about: financing, PHARE, Know-How Funds, it's all over my head. Instead I look over the latest Presidency paper and start fiddling with my earpiece. The Presidency rings the bell and the Council reconvenes. The President runs through an introductory spiel about the search for agreement and the need for a spirit of compromise, the Commissioner mumbles something in reply, and it all starts in earnest. Just as predicted, most Member States intervene to praise the Presidency compromise and lift their remaining reserves. All seems to be going well.

Then the Finns raise the camel problem. A ripple of fear runs through the room. Attachés shimmer around behind the Ministers, trying to repair the common position.

The President then produces the compromise. One Minister calls for solidarity, others raise their eyes to heaven or mutter darkly. Then our Minister intervenes to say that the UK too had some reservations, but the proposal is vital and when it comes to swallowing something awkward, ostriches do it all the time, so why can't we?

Uproar, laughter ripples round as the joke passes through the interpretation, and the Finnish Minister agrees to enter a minutes statement on camels. The President concludes that there is unanimity on the common position. Everyone breaks into applause, a happy buzz fills the room, smiles all round. The Minister thanks me before turning his mind to the next item.

My colleagues start drifting towards the bar. The press attaché ask me to explain the deal to the specialist journalists downstairs. Then I return to the delegation room, have a quick word with Pete Wagers about the telegram reporting this triumph to Whitehall, and that's it. Mission over.

Of course, by then I'm too late to get a room at the Europa (Phil's snaffled that), but Sue from UKRep suggests a cheaper, better alternative. One could almost come to enjoy this negotiating lark.

**8 p.m.** I wander back to the bar, where the others are unwinding. I'm a bit tired by then, but feel I should stay. Across the room I spot Malcolm Bleat, who's talking to a charming woman who seems to be really interested in what he's saying. That's odd, because at parties Malcolm always ends up going on about bathing water policy. But she's even got out a microphone to tape what he has to say.

Sitting round with my colleagues, as the drinks flow, we chat, swap anecdotes, confess our most devious negotiating ploys to each other. Will I be able to remember any of this in the morning? I hope not.

I end up talking to my Danish colleague.

'I love these animals. You must believe this,' she says. I nod, in a way I hope looks believing. 'Rhinos and pangolins: they are my life. So today I am very, very happy. We drink to this, *ja*?' We drink. It's Aquavit, so I think the top of my head is off into orbit. 'But this deal, you know. What of tomorrow? What will the Parliament make of it, eh? Tell me that!'

Depressing thoughts. Time to go. I weave back to the delegation room. All is quiet. Sue is still knitting. The other UKRep attaché is laying down the law to some Deputy-Secretary from Cabinet Office. Business as usual. I collect my coat and bags just as the experts for tomorrow's items arrive. The Council goes on.

## 2 April

Over breakfast on the Eurostar back to London, I look through the European section of the *FT*. News about my Council has been relegated by coverage of the Cream Tea Crisis entering its third week. There's a report on the Tea-pots Directive, questioning whether it will actually come into effect that quickly, but nothing much on my dossier, except a jokey piece about Euro-sloths.

Never mind. I tuck into my breakfast, glad to be heading

home and remembering yesterday's vile breakfast, when the toast comes with some bizarre muck called 'Stone The Crows You'd Need A Laboratory To Tell It Apart From Marmalade!'

# Appendix I
# Checklists

*We're sitting on the plane. The first working group meeting on our dossier is tomorrow morning. So do we sit back, relax and call out for more BA-style champagne? Or do we think of the pilot, who even now is checking that everything is in place and working, that all the necessary preparations have been made, and that the plane has enough engines, wings and cold collations to make it through to Brussels? Do we do the same, and pull out these tedious but vital checklists for one last read through?*

*Yes, I'm afraid we do. But, naturally, we first make sure there's a bottle of bubbly to hand.*

## Introduction

Negotiating in Brussels is a complicated, drawn-out and unpredictable business, rarely following a smooth, clear path. This makes it is easy to overlook tasks or points which need consideration. Hence the idea of checklists: those reproduced here cover six points in the negotiating process, from the first suggestion for action in an area from the Commission, through the practical steps to take in preparing for negotiations; the adoption of a proposal by the Commission; the negotiations in the Council working groups; and the preparation for Council itself. Some are aimed specifically at civil servants, but all should help you and your team to plan, discuss and assign tasks.

## Checklist A: When Action is First Proposed

1. Why has the Commission proposed action in this area?
2. Who supports the need for action (Member States, Non-

Governmental Organisations, public opinion, recent scientific findings)?

3. Who will be affected by the proposed legislation? Central and local government? Companies? Sectional interests? Individuals? What are their views?

4. Are their views realistic and well-judged or are they overstated and/or based on unwarranted fears?

5. What action has the Community already taken in this field? Have other bodies such as the OECD or the UN acted or planned to act?

6. Where does UK domestic policy stand? How well does the proposal fit with UK Government policy?

7. Is there, at first sight, a case for Community action?

## Checklist B: Before Negotiations Begin

1. Who needs to be alerted and copied in on papers? Other parts of the organisation? Other groups? Who in Whitehall?

2. Should a consultative group be set up? Could these groups be mobilised to help to influence the Commission and other Member States?

3. Have you considered the background to the negotiations with lawyers?

4. What resources will be needed during the negotiations? Are additional staff required?

5. Are all the members of the negotiation team identified and up to speed?

6. What are the views of governments and interested parties in other Member States? Do you have natural allies? Is there support for your position?

## Checklist C: Commission Proposal Drafted

1. Is the proposal in an appropriate legal form (Regulation, Directive or Recommendation) and with an acceptable legal base?

2. Is the proposal consistent in itself and with other legislation?

3. What are the implications of the proposal for domestic legislation and practice?

4. To what extent does it meet your objectives?

5. Does it contain provisions which pose problems? Transposition period? Coverage of the Channel Islands and Gibraltar?

6. Is it compatible with Article 3b of the Treaty? (subsidiarity)

7. What burdens, including costs, does it place on the individual, business and government (both central and local)? Are these proportional to the benefits the proposal should bring? (deregulation)

8. What powers are delegated to the Commission? (comitology)

9. How much would it cost to implement the proposal?

10. If the proposal is based on scientific, statistical or other research, do the figures hold up? Have you checked with the appropriate experts?

## Checklist D: Proposal Adopted by the Commission (Civil Servants only)

1. Have you submitted an Explanatory Memorandum to the Westminster Parliament?

2. Have you drafted briefing for the European Parliament?

3. Is some kind of formal response to the proposal, such as a Non-paper (a semi-formal statement of Government policy) appropriate?

4. Have you assessed the need to supply colleagues, including EU Posts and UKRep, with background briefing on the proposal and, where appropriate, a line to take?

5. What further meetings are needed with other Member States?

6. What will be the external costs (to industry, local government, etc)? Are they proportionate to the perceived benefits of action?

7. Have you completed a Compliance Cost Assessment (CCA)? Have the Commission assessed the costs of implementation, both for the Community budget and in Member

States?

8. Have you considered how the proposal would be implemented?

9. Have you put the issues raised to Ministers?


## Checklist E: As Negotiations Progress

1. Have you recently reassessed your own negotiating strength?

2. Are you on course to achieve your overall objective? If not, how might you modify your objectives?

3. Are there negotiating points of marginal importance to use as bargaining chips?

4. What are the key points for other Member States? Could you offer support in return for help with your own concerns?


## Checklist F: Proposal goes to Council (for Civil Servants)

1. Has the proposal cleared Parliamentary scrutiny?

2. Has the UK negotiating position been cleared around Whitehall?

3. Have you discussed the outline of the Council brief with UKRep?

4. Is the brief itself on course to be completed and cleared with other Government departments well before the Council?

5. Who will attend to brief the Minister?

6. Should a lawyer be present?

7. Are the other key team members contactable by phone/fax (24 hours)?

8. Have you amassed the necessary papers?

9. Have you checked the latest Secretariat texts for Council for any last-minute, unheralded amendments or other hidden horrors?

10. Have you checked your arrangements? Flights, hotel booking, foreign currency? Is your passport still valid?

## Checklist G: Before Leaving the Council (for Civil Servants)

1. Before leaving the Council, do you have all the papers which make up the common position or other agreement?
2. Have you prepared a contribution for the Parliamentary Question reporting the outcome of the Council?
3. Have you given your press officer and/or the UKRep press attaché a brief on the outcome and a line to take?
4. Have you discussed the reporting telegram with UKRep?
5. Finally, is the well-deserved champagne on ice?

# Appendix II
# Abbreviations and Acronyms

*Apparently, there are more European Union acronyms than there are atoms in the universe. Here is a selection.*

| | |
|---|---|
| ACP | African, Caribbean and Pacific parties to the Lomé Convention |
| AOB | Any Other Business |
| ARC | Rainbow Group of the European Parliament |
| AT | *Agent Temporaire* |
| BENELUX | Customs Union of Belgium, the Netherlands and Luxembourg |
| CAP | Common Agricultural Policy |
| CCA | Compliance Cost Assessment |
| CCP | Common Commercial Policy |
| CCT | Common Customs Tariff |
| CEC | Commission of the European Community |
| CEDEFOP | European Centre for the Development of Vocational Training |
| CEEC | Countries of Central and Eastern Europe |
| CEN | European Committee for Standardisation |
| CENELEC | European Committee for Electrotechnical Standardisation |
| CERD | European Committee for Research and Development |
| CFP | Common Fisheries Policy |
| CFSP | Common Foreign and Security Policy |
| COLA | Cabinet Office Legal Advisers |
| COPA | Committee for Agricultural Organisations in the EU |
| COR | Committee of the Regions |

| | |
|---|---|
| CLS | Commission (occasionally Council) Legal Service |
| COREPER | Committee of Permanent Representatives |
| DG | Directorate-General; Director-General |
| DNE | Detached National Expert |
| DOM | *Département D'outremer* |
| DOT | Department of Transport |
| DPR | Deputy Permanent Representative |
| DTI | Department of Trade and Industry |
| EAEC | European Atomic Energy Community |
| EAGGF | European Agricultural Guidance and Guarantee Fund (also FEOGA) |
| EBRD | European Bank for Reconstruction and Development |
| EC | European Community |
| ECHR | European Court of Human Rights |
| ECJ | European Court of Justice |
| ECSC | European Coal and Steel Community |
| ECU | European Currency Unit |
| EEC | European Economic Community |
| ECOFIN | Economics and Finance Council |
| ECPA | European Centre for Public Affairs |
| EEA | European Economic Area |
| EFTA | European Free Trade Association |
| EIB | European Investment Bank |
| EIF | European Investment Fund |
| EM | Explanatory Memorandum |
| EMEA | European Medicines Evaluation Agency |
| EMI | European Monetary Institute |
| EMS | European Monetary System |
| EMU | Economic and Monetary Union |
| EP | European Parliament |
| EPLP | European Parliamentary Labour Party |
| EPO | European Patent Office |
| EPP | European People's Party |
| EQ(O) | European Questions (Officials) Committee |
| EQ(O)L | European Questions (Officials) |

|  | (Lawyers) Committee |
| EQ(S) | European Questions (Senior Officials) Committee |
| ERDF | European Regional Development Fund |
| ESA | European Space Agency |
| ESC | Economic and Social Committee |
| ESF | European Social Fund |
| EU | European Union |
| EUD(I)/(E) | European Union Department (Internal)/(External), FCO |
| EURATOM | European Atomic Energy Community |
| EUROCONTROL | European Organisation for the Safety of Air Navigation |
| EUROPES | European Public Expenditure Survey (UK Government spending controls) |
| EUROSTAT | European Statistical office |
| FCO | Foreign and Commonwealth Office |
| FEOGA | European Agricultural Guidance and Guarantee Fund |
| FIFG | Financial Instrument for Fisheries Guidance |
| HSE | Health and Safety Executive |
| IGC | Inter-Governmental Conference |
| JRC | Joint Research Centre, Ispra, Italy |
| MAFF | Ministry of Agriculture, Fisheries and Food |
| MEP | Member of the European Parliament |
| NATO | North Atlantic Treaty Organisation |
| NGO | Non-Governmental Organisations |
| OECD | Organisation for Economic Co-operation and Development |
| OGDs | Other Government Departments |
| OJ | Official Journal of the European Union |
| PES | Party of European Socialists or Public Expenditure Survey (UK) |
| PQ | Parliamentary Question |

| | |
|---|---|
| QMV | Qualified Majority Voting |
| SEA | Single European Act |
| SME | Small and Medium Enterprises |
| TEN | Trans-European Network |
| TOM | *Territoire D'outremer* |
| TGV | *Train à Grande Vitesse* |
| UKRep | UK Representation to the European Union |
| UN | United Nations |
| UNECE | United Nations Economic Commission for Europe |
| UNEP | United Nations Environment Programme |
| UNICE | Union of Industries in the European Community (employers' group) |
| VAT | Value Added Tax |
| WEU | Western European Union |
| WHO | World Health Organisation |
| WTO | World Trade Organisation |

# Appendix III
# Sources of Further Information

There is a huge amount of information available on the European Union and its works, and every day thousands more pages flood out. This Appendix concentrates on how to navigate across this paper ocean, including who to turn to for advice. It covers various **sources of information**, including EU documentation centres, and computer databases. It lists the addresses of **European Commission offices** in each Member State, the Brussels-based **Representations of the Member States** to the EU, and the addresses of the other main **Community institutions**.

These offices will be happy to offer what advice and assistance they can, given the constraints of time and resources, but only to those who help themselves. In other words, before you trouble a Permanent Representation or MEP's office, do all you can to find the information yourself from the sources below.


## European Union Documents

Most central or county libraries will hold complete sets of the *Official Journal* and various other useful documents and leaflets. They should also be able to steer you towards three networks – the European Information, Documentation and Reference Centres – and specialists such as the Law Society and the Confederation of British Industry.

*European Information Centres*
Unlike public libraries, these centres will usually be able to deal with enquiries by phone and also provide services such as advice for small and medium-sized enterprises, advice for businesses looking to expand abroad, and information on company law and taxation. They may also provide documents, usually for a small charge. Most are run by business groups such as chambers of commerce.

*European Documentation Centres*
These are aimed more towards the academic community and most are based in universities, but will usually try to help members of the public or steer them towards other sources of assistance.

*European References Centres*
These are very similar to documentation centres, but only offer a reference service.

*The Law Society*
The Law Society holds lists of solicitors specialising in various fields of European law, and also provides specialist and general guidance through publications and seminars. The Library staff can answer enquiries on European law by phone, fax, letter or in person. The address is 113 Chancery Lane, London WC2A 1PL. Tel: 0171 242 1222. Fax: 0171 831 0344. The Brussels office is at boulevard du regent 58, B-1000 Brussels, Belgium. Tel: (32 2) 502 2020.

*The Confederation of British Industry (CBI)*
The CBI provides information and advice on European affairs to its membership and also to others, including leaflets, briefing sheets, and even a video. It also runs conferences and seminars, and publishes a fortnightly faxed news-sheet on European policy issues (CBI members only) called *Eurowire*. The CBI address is: Centre Point, 103 New Oxford Street, London WC1A 1DU. Tel: 0171 379 7400. The CBI office in Brussels is at: rue Joseph II 40 (bte 1), B-1000 Brussels, Belgium. Tel: (32 2) 231 0465. Fax: 230 9832.

## Electronic Media and the Internet

There are a number of databases with useful information available on-line or on computer disk (CD-ROM). If your resources can run to it, the most effective way to keep informed is to subscribe to an on-line information service (what was once known as a 'wire service') such as the Reuters European service. This sends news and information twenty-four hours a day on everything from invitations to tender for Community projects to the latest news from the

European Council, all direct to your computer terminal. You can search the database by subject, date, or by looking for key words in the text of the articles.

The most extreme gizmo you might consider is **CELEX**: the legal database of the EC. It contains the text of all legislative acts (though when you print it out the text splurges all over the page and so isn't as easy to read or use as the OJ). Best of all, you can search for texts by key words, reference numbers or by the title. CELEX is available on subscription either on-line or on high-capacity computer disk (CD-ROM).

There are also three Internet sites of interest:

*EUROPA: http://www.cec.lu*
(information on objectives and policies: widely used, with over 80,000 'hits' (users) each day)

*I'M EUROPE: http://www.echo.lu*
(information for researchers)

*EUROBASES*
(text of the *Official Journal*, press notices, etc). Available by subscription only from EUROBASES. Fax: (352) 2929 42025.


## The European Commission

The Commission has offices (representations) in each capital city of the Member States, and other major cities, and in many other countries across the world. These offices both represent the European Commission and the Union as a whole, providing information and promoting objectives and policies to the citizens and the national and local government of the host Member State. They also feed information back to the Commission, to help inform its decision-making.

Each office also briefs the media on European stories and answers enquiries from the public.

The European Commission Representation to the UK is at 8 Storey's Gate, London SW1P 3AT. Tel: 0171 973 1992. Fax: 0171 973 1900.

There are also Commission offices in Scotland, Wales and Northern Ireland:

9 Alva Street, Edinburgh EH2 4P. Tel: 0131 225 2058. Fax: 0131 226 4105.

4 Cathedral Road, Cardiff CF1 9SG. Tel: 01222 371631. Fax: 01222 395489.

Windsor House, 9/15 Bedford Street, Belfast, BT2 7EG. Tel: 01232 240708. Fax: 01232 248241.

## European Commission Representations to the Member States

| | |
|---|---|
| Austria: | Hoyosgasse 5, AT-1040 Wien. Tel: (43) 1 505 3379. |
| Belgium: | Rue Archimède 73, B-1040 Brussels. Tel: (32) 2 295 3844. |
| Denmark: | Ostergade 61, Postbok 144, 1004 Copenhagen K. Tel: (45) 33 14 41 40. |
| Finland: | Pohjoisesplanadi 1, FIN-00131 Helsinki. Tel: (358) 0 65 64 20. |
| France: | 288 blvd St Germain, 75007 Paris. Tel: (33) 1 40 63 38 00. |
| | 2, rue Henri-Barbusse, 13241 Marseille. Tel: (33) 91 91 46 00. |
| Germany: | Zitelmannstrasse 22, D-53106 Bonn. Tel: (49) 22853 00 90. |
| | Kurfurstendamm 102, D-10711 Berlin. Tel: (49) 30896 09 30. |
| | Erhardstrasse 27, D-80331 München. Tel: (49) 89202 10 11. |
| Greece: | 2 Vassilissis Sofias, Case Postale 11002, Athens. Tel: (30) 1 725 1000. |
| Ireland: | 39 Molesworth Street, Dublin 2. Tel: (353) 1 671 2244. |
| Italy: | Via Poli 29, 00187 Rome. Tel: (39) 6 699 1160. |
| | Corso Magenta 59, 20123 Milan. Tel: (39) 2 4801 2505. |
| Luxembourg: | Rue Alcide De Gasperi, 2920 Luxembourg. Tel: (352) 430 11. |

Netherlands:    Korte Vijverberg 5, 2513 AB The Hague. Tel: (31) 70 346 93 26.

Portugal:    Largo Jean Monnet 1–10, 1200 Lisbon. Tel: (351) 1 350 9800.

Spain:    C/Serrano 41, 28001 Madrid. Tel: (34) 1 435 1700.

Av Diagonal 407 bis, Planta 18, 08008 Barcelona. Tel: (34) 3 415 81 77.

Sweden:    Hamnagatan 6, Box 7323, S-10390 Stockholm. Tel: (46) 8 611 1172.

## Selected External European Commission Representations

Australia:
18 Arkana Street, Yarralumla, ACT 2600, Canberra. Tel: (61 6) 271 2777. Fax: 273 4445.

Hong Kong:
19/F St John's Building, 33 Garden Road, Central, Hong Kong. Tel: (852) 2537 6083. Fax: 2522 1302.

India:
65 Golf Links, New Delhi 111 003. Tel: (91 11) 462 9237. Fax: 462 9206.

Israel:
The Tower, 17th floor, 3 Daniel Frisch Street, Tel Aviv 64731. Tel: (972 3) 696 4166. Fax: 695 1983.

Norway:
Haakon VII's gate 6, N-0161 Oslo. Tel: (47) 22 83 35 83. Fax: 22 83 40 55.

Pakistan:
House No. 9, Street No. 88, Sector G-6/3, Islamabad. Tel: (92 51) 27 18 28. Fax: 82 26 04.

Russia:
Pevchesky Pereulok 2/10, 109028 Moscow. Tel: (7 592) 20 46 58. Fax: 220 4654.

South Africa:
2 Green Park Estates, 27 George Storrar Drive, Groenkloof,
Pretoria 0181. Tel: (27 12) 46 43 49. Fax: 46 99 23.
64 Keerom Street, Cape Town 8001. Tel: (27 21) 23 03 05.
Fax: 23 03 27.

United States:
2300 M Street NW, Washington, DC 20037. Tel: (202) 862
9500. Fax: 429 1766.
3 Dag Hammarskjold Plaza, 305 East 47th Street, New York,
NY 10017. Tel: (212) 371 3804. Fax: 758 2718.


## Addresses of the main European Union Institutions

### Committee of the Regions
Rue Belliard 79
B-1040 Brussels
Tel: (32 2) 282 2211
Fax: (32 2) 282 2085

### Council of the European Union
Rue de la Loi 175
B-1048 Brussels
Tel: (32 2) 285 6111
Fax: (32 2) 285 7397

### Court of Auditors
12 rue Alcide de Gasperi
L-1615 Luxembourg
Tel: (352) 43 981

### Economic and Social Committee
Rue Ravenstein 2
B-1000 Brussels
Tel: (32 2) 519 9011
Fax: (32 2) 513 4893

### European Commission
Rue de la Loi 200
B-1049 Brussels
Tel: (32 2) 299 1111

*(Note: this is a postal address only. The Commission offices*

*are spread around Brussels and even Luxembourg so for meetings you should check the exact address.)*

**European Court of Justice**
Boulevard Konrad Adenauer
L-2925 Luxembourg
Tel: (352) 43 981

**European Investment Bank**
100 boulevard Konrad Adenauer
L-2950 Luxembourg
Tel: (352) 43 791

**European Parliament (MEPs' Offices)**
97–113 rue Belliard
B-1047 Brussels
Tel: (32 2) 284 2111
Fax: (32 2) 284 6933

**European Parliament (Plenary Sessions)**
Palais de l'Europe
F-67006 Strasbourg
Tel: (33) 1 88 17 40 01
Fax: (33) 1 88 25 65 01

**European Parliament (Secretariat)**
Centre Européen, Plateau de Kirchberg
L-2929 Luxembourg
Tel: (352) 43 001
Fax: (352) 43 7009

**European Parliament (UK Office)**
2 Queen Anne's Gate
London SW1H 9AA
Tel: 0171 227 4300
Fax: 0171 227 4301 (Library) and 4302 (General)

**Permanent Representations of the Member States to the European Union**

*(All offices are in Brussels. The prefix for Belgium is 32 and for Brussels is 2).*

Austria:  Avenue de Cortenbergh 118, B-1040. Tel: 741 2111. Fax: 735 8347.

Belgium:  Rue Belliard 62, B-1040. Tel: 233 2111.

|              | Fax: 233 1075. |
|--------------|----------------|
| Denmark:     | Rue d'Arlon 73, B-1040. Tel: 233 0811. Fax: 230 9384. |
| Finland:     | Rue des Tréves 100, B-1040. Tel: 287 8411. Fax: 287 8400. |
| France:      | Place de Louvain 14, B-1000. Tel: 229 8211. Fax: 229 8262. |
| Germany:     | Rue J de Lalaing 19–21, B-1040. Tel: 238 1811. Fax: 238 1978. |
| Greece:      | Rue Montoyer 25, B-1040. Tel: 551 5611. Fax: 551 5651. |
| Ireland:     | Avenue Galilée 5, Boite 22, B-1030. Tel: 218 0605. Fax: 218 1347. |
| Italy:       | Rue du Marteau 9, B-1040. Tel: 220 0411. Fax: 219 3449. |
| Luxembourg:  | Rue du Noyer 211, B-1040. Tel: 735 2060. Fax: 736 1429. |
| Netherlands: | Avenue Hermann Debroux 48, B-1160. Tel: 679 1511. Fax: 679 1775. |
| Portugal:    | Rue Marie-Thérèse 11–13, B-1000. Tel: 227 4200. Fax: 218 1542. |
| Spain:       | Boulevard du Régent 52, B-1000. Tel: 509 8611. Fax: 511 1940. |
| Sweden:      | Square de Meeûs 30, B-1000. Tel: 289 5611. Fax: 289 5600. |
| UK:          | Avenue d'Audergham 10, B-1040. Tel: 287 8211. Fax: 287 8397. |

## Study and Training in European Affairs

The Civil Service College, Sunningdale, Ascot, Berkshire SL5 OQE. Tel: 01344 634206. Fax: 01344 634091.

European Centre for Public Affairs, Templeton College, Oxford OX1 SNY. Tel: 01865 735422. Fax: 736374.

# Appendix IV
# Glossary of French Terms

| | |
|---|---|
| Agent temporaire | Commission employee on a contract |
| Carnet | Book of 10 Brussels metro tickets. |
| Chef de cabinet | Head of a Commissioner's private staff |
| Contre-filet | Double safety-net (Regulatory Committee Type IIIb) |
| Concertation sur place | Co-ordination at the site of an international meeting |
| Fiche | One-page summary of an infraction case |
| Fiche d'impact | Assessment of the financial implications of a proposal |
| Filet | Safety-net (Regulatory Committee Type IIIa) |
| Fonctionnaire | Member of permanent staff of the Commission (civil servant) |
| Hebdomadaire | Weekly (meetings) |
| Huissiers | Staff who manage the meeting-rooms, circulate documents, etc. |
| Limité | Document with limited circulation |
| Mutualité | Compulsory private insurance scheme |
| Navette | Process of budget consultation between Council and Parliament |
| Rapporteur | The MEP who prepares a report for an EP committee |
| Restraint | Document with restricted circulation |
| Salle d'écoute | Room where Council proceedings are relayed |
| Stagiaire | Employee on short-term (5-month) work experience |

# Index